THE LALA PRINCIPLES

Timeless Business Wisdom From The Baniya Mindset

THE LALA PRINCIPLES

Timeless Business Wisdom From The Baniya Mindset

NITIN GUPTA

Available on amazonkindle

Worldwide Published by

Pendown Press

PREMIUM BUSINESS PUBLISHER

PENDOWN PRESS LLP

An ISO 9001 & ISO 14001 Certified Co.,

Regd. Office: 3767A, Kanhaiya Nagar,
Tri Nagar, Delhi-110035

Ph.: 8130886000, 9650072927

E-mail: info@pendownpress.com

Branch Office: 1A/2A, 20, Hari Sadan, Ansari Road,
Daryaganj, New Delhi-110002

Ph.: 011-45794768

Website: PendownPress.com

Edition: 2024

Price: ₹ 499

ISBN: 978-93-6338-025-7

Layout and Cover Designed by Pendown Graphics Team

Printed and Bound in India by Thomson Press India Ltd.

DEDICATION

To my beloved parents and mentors, your guidance, values, and unwavering belief in me have shaped every step of this journey.

And to the resilient ***'Baniya'*** community, this is a tribute to your timeless spirit of enterprise.

For generations, you've been the architects of India's commerce, building not just businesses but entire ecosystems of trust, trade, and transformation.

Your instincts for value, your dedication to relationships, and your unshakeable work ethic have lit the path for countless entrepreneurs, including me.

You've shown that building a business is not just about profit, but about purpose, persistence.

This book honors the legacy you've created and the future this community is building.

Table of Contents

Acknowledgements

With deep gratitude, I thank my family; your love, patience, and belief in me have been my constant anchor. Before anything else, before any business principle, strategy, or success —

There was **sacrifice**, **discipline**, **faith**, and **family**.

To my father, Sh. Kamal Prakash Gupta

Thank you for showing me what real hard work looks like.

You didn't just run a business; you built a legacy with your sweat, your sincerity, and your silent strength.

Your life taught me that **commitment is louder than words** — and that integrity is non-negotiable.

To my mother, Smt. Anita Devi

Thank you for being the emotional backbone of our family. Your support, patience, and silent prayers carried me through the toughest times. From you, I learned that **success is not just about doing well — it's about staying grounded while doing so.**

To my Chacha Ji

You've been more than an uncle — you've been a teacher, a partner, and a role model.

To my father-in-law

He was a well-known name in the transport industry. His guidance to be disciplined and to achieve anything with hard work was priceless. **"NOT POSSIBLE"** was not in his dictionary. The only thing needed to succeed is to keep your intentions positive, for all is what I have learnt from him.

To my mother-in-law

Thank you for teaching us to be simple, loving, productive, and forward-thinking. Your time management & smart money-saving skills have made a lasting impact on our lives.

To my siblings

You've been my first competitors, supporters, teachers, and best friends — all at once.

Growing up with you in a joint family wasn't just a blessing; it was **an everyday masterclass in leadership, ambition, and the will to outdo ourselves.**

Thank you for always pushing me, challenging me, and believing in me — even when I doubted myself.

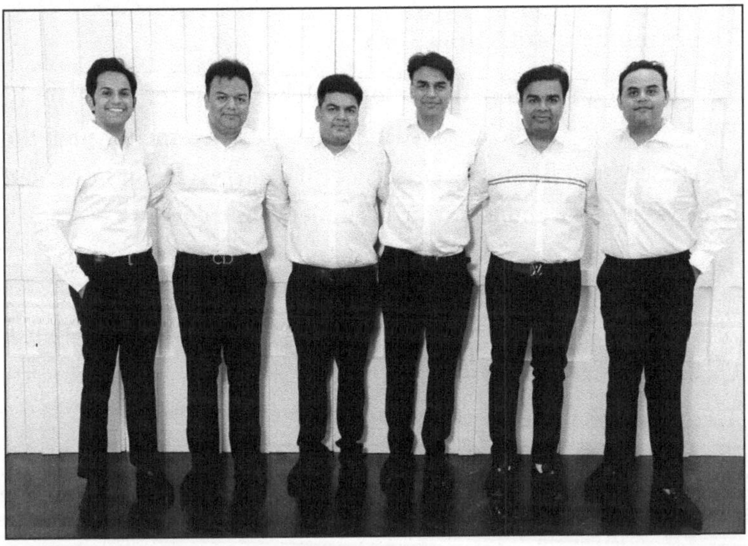

To all my family members

Thank you for being my roots and my wings.

Your values have shaped my character.

Your faith has given me strength.

Your presence has made my life rich, not just in success, but in meaning, belonging, and love.

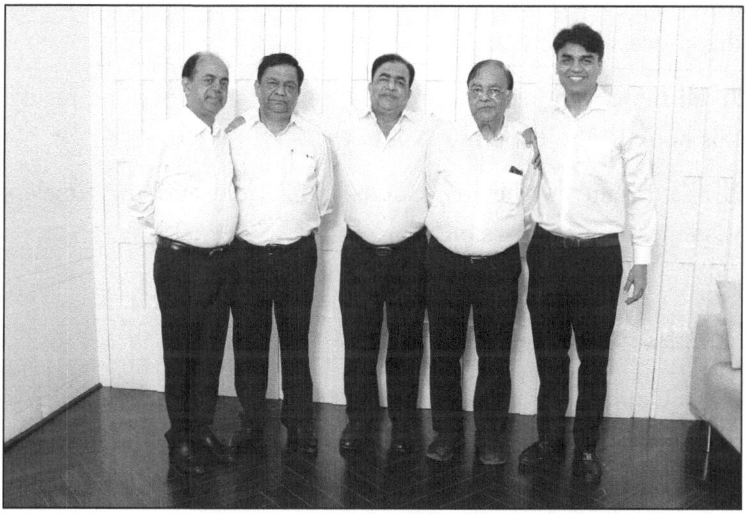

To my ancestors

I bow my head in respect to the generations that came before me.

Their values, their principles, their stories — some spoken, some silently lived — are the foundation on which my identity stands.

The *LALA Principles* are not new; they are **your teachings**, passed down through time, now written in words.

To my friends

You stood by me in moments of doubt and cheered for me in

moments of clarity. Thank you for your faith.

A heartfelt thanks to every mentor

You shaped my journey through sharing your time, wisdom, and insights with me.

Sincere gratitude to Dinesh Verma

The CEO of Pendown Press, my publishers, and his excellent team for guiding and supporting me at every step, and making this process smooth and joyful.

To all those who believed in this vision before it became reality, this book is not just mine — it is **yours.**

It is a tribute to the life lessons I inherited and the timeless wisdom I hope to pass on.

With love, reverence, and unending gratitude,

Nitin Gupta

Preface

"You don't need a business background to be a great entrepreneur—you need the right values."

In a world filled with constant noise and unending distraction, clarity and intention have become rare treasures. The LALA Principles arrive at a time when we need them most—a guide, a compass, and a challenge to live differently.

Rooted in simplicity yet profound in impact, these principles invite us to reconnect with what matters, to live, act, learn, and adapt with purpose.

This book isn't just a set of ideas. It's a mindset.
A way of being.

Whether you're a leader, creator, student, or seeker, the LALA Principles offer more than just theory—they offer transformation. Page by page, the reader is encouraged to slow down, listen deeply, reflect honestly, and move forward with courage.

As you begin this journey, I invite you to approach these pages not as a checklist, but as a conversation. One that challenges and nurtures. One that speaks to the core of who you are—and who you are becoming.

Welcome to The LALA Principles. May they serve you well…

The content in this book is all about the genuine thought process and the inherent business acumen of our Business *"Baniya"* community.

The terms **"Baniya"** *&* **"Lala"** carry many interpretations, often clouded by stereotypes. But to me, they represent a deep legacy of entrepreneurship, sharp business instincts, and value-based living.

Having grown up in a *Baniya* household and later ventured into the startup world, I found myself constantly drawing from this treasure trove of wisdom.

This book is written with the intention to decode and share those principles, drawing parallels between traditional business thinking and the modern startup ecosystem.

I call them the LALA Principles—not just because of the colloquial term often used for business owners (though I am proud of that heritage too), but because each letter reflects core business values:

- L: Loyalty to Business
- A: Accounting and Financial Prudence
- L: Life-long Learning
- A: Adapting to Changing Needs & Times

Here's a peek into the Timeless LALA Sayings that form the foundation of this book, and will assist you as solid pillars to build your business skyscraper.

1. ***"Dhandha sirf munafa nahi, vishwas ka bhi khel hai."***

   ("Business is not just about profit — it's a game of trust.")

2. ***"Jo baat keh di, woh patthar ki lakeer samjho."***

   ("A word once given is as firm as a line etched in stone.")

3. ***"Grahak bhagwan hai–lekin bhagwan ko bhi seva chahiye."***

   ("The customer is God–but even God expects devotion.")

4. ***"Samay pe maal dena izzat ka sawaal hai."***

   ("Timely delivery is a matter of honor.")

5. ***"Bina mehnat ke na Lakshmi tikti hai, na dosti."***

   ("Without hard work, neither wealth nor relationships last.")

6. ***"Jo bazaar ki baat sunta hai, wahi asli vakil hota hai apne product ka."***

   ("He who listens to the market becomes the best advocate for his product.")

7. ***"Paise ki izzat karo, paisa tumhari karega."***

   ("Respect money, and money will respect you back.")

8. ***"Udhaar sirf wahan do jahan bharosa ho — aur hisaab pakka ho."***

   ("Offer credit only where there is trust — and clear accounting.")

9. ***"Kamao kam, sikka jama karo zyada."***

   ("Even if profits are less, build your credibility more.")

10. ***"Naye zamane ke tareeke seekho — lekin apne sanskaar mat bhoolo."***

    ("Learn the ways of the new world — but never forget your values.")

Know Your Author

Nitin Gupta was born and raised in the bustling lanes of Delhi, surrounded by the nurturing embrace of a traditional Baniya joint family. His story is not just about entrepreneurial success—it is a reflection of deep-rooted values, passed down through generations, grounded in simplicity, integrity, and unwavering hard work.

He grew up in a household where over thirty family members still live together—a rare and beautiful testament to unity, shared responsibilities, and the quiet strength of tradition. Watching his father and uncles rise from humble beginnings to earn deep respect in society left a lasting impression on him. Their journey, built on grit, resilience, and trust, became his first and most powerful business school—teaching him lessons no institution ever could.

Lala Principles was born from this lived experience. It is not a theoretical playbook—it is a heartfelt collection of values, real-life observations, and ethical practices, absorbed through years of watching, doing, and reflecting. These are the principles that shaped Nitin's worldview and served as the compass for building and leading his own ventures with both courage and conscience.

In writing this book, Nitin hopes to honor the timeless wisdom of those who came before him and to share these time-tested foundations with aspiring entrepreneurs. He believes that true business success is never measured by profits alone—but by purpose, perseverance, and the lives we uplift along the way.

This book is his tribute—to the spirit of the "Lala," to the enduring power of family, and to every reader who chooses to lead with values.

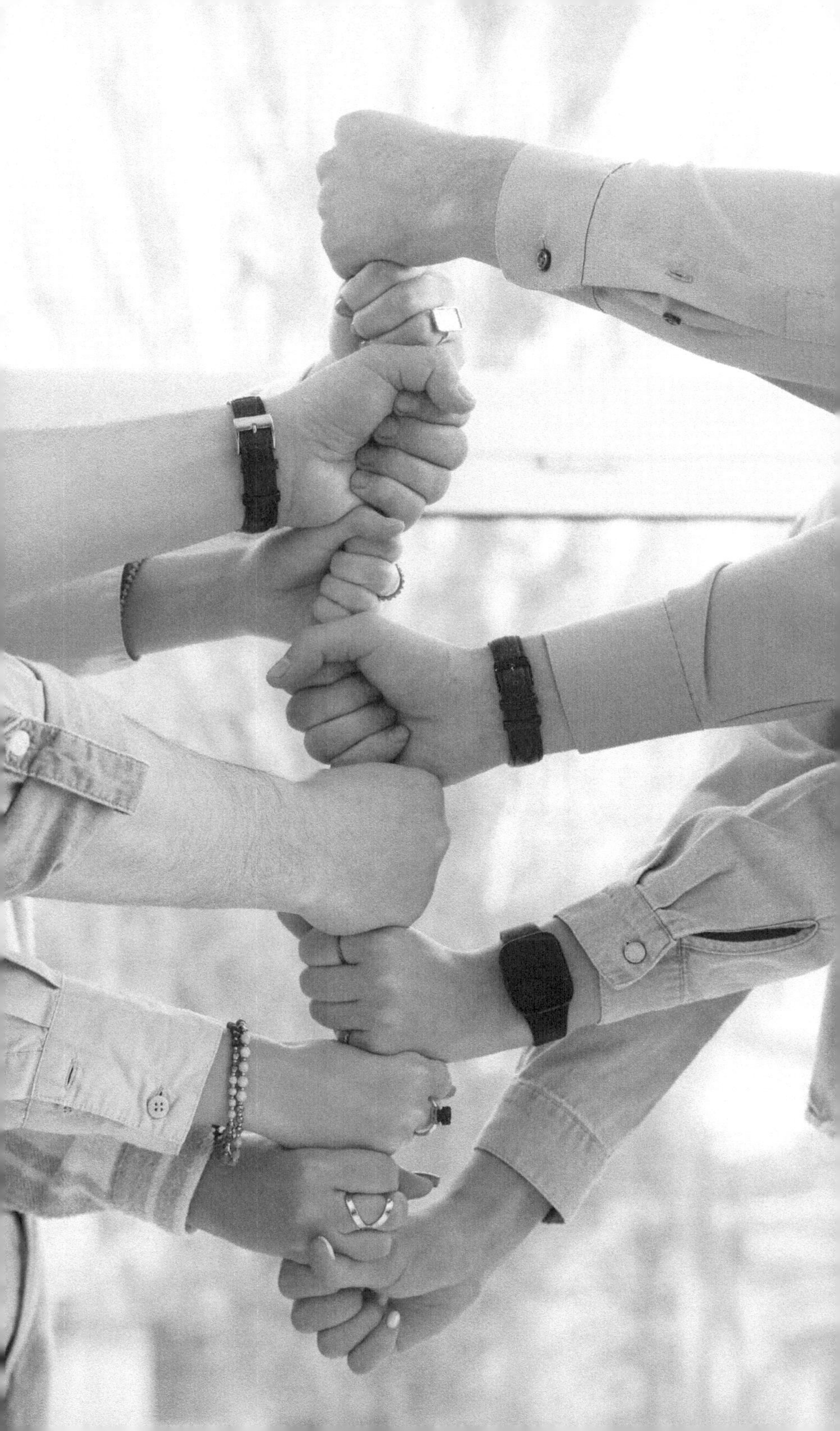

SEGMENT 1
The Foundation

This opening section lays the groundwork for *The **LALA** Principles,* a business philosophy rooted in timeless values and real-world wisdom, inspired by the ***Baniya*** way of life.

In a world chasing speed, scale, and shortcuts, **The Foundation** brings us back to what truly matters: integrity, relationships, frugality, and trust. It explores why these principles, often passed down through generations, are more relevant than ever for today's entrepreneurs.

Here, you'll understand why this book was written, why now, and most importantly, who it's for; from first-time founders and family business successors to values-driven professionals and curious learners.

This section introduces

- The meaning and power of the ***LALA*** mindset — Learn, Apply, Leverage, Adapt.
- The author's personal journey and the cultural roots that shaped his business philosophy.
- A tribute to the Baniya community's role in shaping Indian enterprise and society.

This section is like a meet & greet, a warm welcome, a handshake of trust, and a call to awaken the entrepreneur within, grounded in tradition, ready for the future.

The Foundations of My Strength — Wisdom & Lessons from My Family

In every entrepreneur's life, there are a few **silent forces** working behind the scenes, cheering, correcting, inspiring, and anchoring.

For me, that force has always been **my family**.

My **wife**, my **daughter**, and my **son** — these three are more than family. They are my **idea-generating machines**, my **daily dose of reality and motivation**, and my **reminders of what really matters.**

My Wife — The Wisdom Behind the Action

From the very beginning, my wife has been my **mirror and motivator**. She constantly nudged me to look around, stay alert, and face the truth of what's happening, not just in business, but in life.

She made me understand the true essence of competition.

"Competition is not about tearing others down but about building yourself up."

She taught me that **healthy competition** isn't something to fear; it's a **necessary spice** in life.

It keeps us dynamic, on our toes, always improving, and never getting comfortable.

Her quiet strength and sharp insight made sure I **never stopped moving forward.**

My Daughter — The Shining Star Who Made Me Brave

My daughter was born with a light, a **star** in every sense.

From childhood, she was adventurous, a quick learner, and an academic topper.

She never feared the stage. She **owned it** — grabbing the mic, commanding attention, and sharing her voice with clarity and grace.

I, on the other hand, always had thoughts, but stage fright held me back.

Watching her speak with such confidence, I realized something powerful:

> ***"Everything can be learned — all you need is courage and practice."***

Because of her, I **faced my fear**.

Today, I proudly speak in public, and people now say, *"Let's hear what he has to say."*

This transformation — from fear to leadership — began with the inspiration of **my daughter.**

She continues to be a **leader, a helper, and a light for everyone around her.**

She is truly my *shining star*, and I know her wisdom will light up many lives.

My Son — "Chhota Packet, Bada Dhamaka"

My son is just 12, but his thoughts? Way beyond his years. At the age of 8, he was already talking about things like:

- Savings
- Investment opportunities
- Branding
- Creation

These are not just business terms. They are the **core of the LALA Principles.**

Hearing him speak like that filled me with pride, not just as a father, but as a lifelong learner myself.

He is already a **superstar in my eyes**, and I know with God's blessings and his clarity, he will go far and **spread knowledge wherever he goes.**

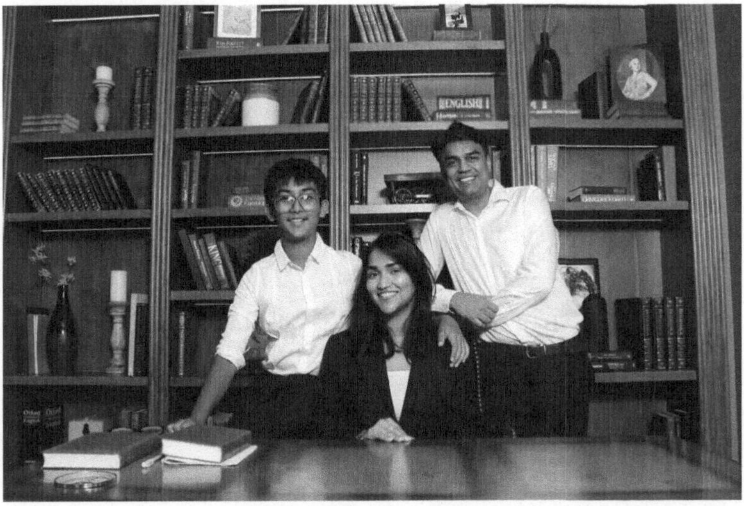

Our "Buddy" — A Masterclass in Time Management

There's another very special person in our life — someone my wife and I affectionately call **"Buddy."**

She runs a successful business, and she taught us one of the most **important tools of the LALA mindset**:

Time Management.

We've seen her **value every minute**, using her day with intention and focus.

Watching her made me rethink my routine and optimize it completely.

Today, I start my day at **4 AM**.

By **6:30 AM**, I have:

- Delegated all my important work
- Made my daily plan
- And carved out "me-time" to think clearly

It feels like I've **completed my day**, even though time is still on my side.

This discipline has become a winning edge in my life.

Behind every entrepreneur is a family —

And behind every principle, a person who taught it quietly through love, actions, or example.

- My wife gave me realism and resilience.
- My daughter gave me confidence and voice.
- My son gave me insight and enthusiasm.

And our Buddy gave us the **gift of time** — a tool more precious than any investment.

I am not just grateful — I am built by them.

CHAPTER 1

WHY THIS BOOK? WHY NOW?

In a world rushing toward innovation, disruption, and digital revolutions, there is something quietly missing in the noise: **timeless wisdom.** The kind passed down through generations, not taught in business schools, but lived in everyday transactions.

The LALA Principles are exactly that—principles rooted in integrity, relationships, frugality, and trust. Principles that shaped not just businesses, but families, communities, and legacies.

I wrote this book because I believe the Baniya way of doing business—deeply practical, deeply principled—is more relevant than ever today.

At a time when the world is facing trust deficits in institutions, companies, and leadership, the foundational values of-

- Commitment
- Clarity
- Service
- And long-term thinking

can offer entrepreneurs a compass.

This is not a book of theories. It is a book of lived experiences—my own and those of the countless Baniya entrepreneurs I've learned from.

It's a tribute to the wisdom of my father, uncles, and elders, who built businesses with nothing but honesty, hard work, and a sharp mind. It's also a guide for the next generation: for those who are building startups, family businesses, or solo hustles—anyone who believes in building with character.

Why now? Because the world needs to remember that **values are not outdated.** They are assets.

- In an age of speed, integrity slows you down just enough to make the right decision.
- In an age of scale, relationships keep you grounded.
- *And in an age of exit strategies, legacy reminds you that building something worthwhile takes time.*

This book is designed to capture and share the essence of the LALA Principles—Learn, Apply, Leverage, Adapt—and the values behind them, with stories that are real, raw, and relevant.

It's a personal journey, but it's also universal.

Welcome to a world where your **Word is your Bond,** and your **Business is your *'Dharma'*.**

CHAPTER 2

Who is this book for?

This book is for every dreamer who wants to build a business not just for income, but for impact. Whether you're a young entrepreneur with a vision, a second-generation family business owner trying to modernize tradition, or a working professional preparing to break into the world of enterprise, the LALA Principles are your compass.

- **For First-Time Entrepreneurs:** If you're just starting out and feel overwhelmed, this book offers you grounding. These principles will help you avoid common pitfalls and build on timeless fundamentals.
- **For Traditional Business Families:** If you come from a business family and want to bridge the old with the new, you'll find this book relatable and empowering. It helps you modernize without forgetting your roots.
- **For Startup Founders:** If you're navigating scaling, funding, and pivoting, these principles bring focus to what really matters: sustainable value creation, customer loyalty, and financial discipline.
- **For Students and Learners:** Even if you're just curious about entrepreneurship, these stories and lessons will plant seeds that can change your mindset for life.

- **For Anyone Who Values Ethics in Business:** If you believe business should be built on trust, relationships, and resilience, this book is your affirmation.

These are not just principles; they are a way of life: Key Business Principles & Strategies, Beliefs & a Mind-set

> No matter where you come from or what stage you're at, – There's a LALA in you.
> This book helps you awaken it.

CHAPTER 3

Hey, Ready to Meet The 'LALA' Behind The Book?

> ***"Success is not what you have but who you become in the process." - Jim Rohn***

Hello, my name is Nitin Gupta, and this book condenses my journey of invaluable lessons, real-life experiences, struggles, small and big wins, and continued personal growth and transformation.

It's a reflection of my life, my entrepreneurial path, and the values that have guided me every step of the way, as they will guide you through this book.

At 45, I feel like I have lived through centuries of wisdom challenges and transformations, not because of how long I lived, it's because of how deeply I have learned.

It is all thanks to the teachings of my grandparents, parents, paternal and maternal families, countless friends, and mentors that I have turned into the person I am. They stood by me, both during storms and sunshine.

Their guidance and personal experiences helped me face the ups and downs of life and business. Navigating these challenges with their support, I have discovered the true power of commitment, hard work, and an unshakable belief in one's values.

These are not just words; they have been my compass in moments of doubt, my strength during setbacks, and the foundation for everything I have built.

"Business opportunities are like buses, there's always another one coming."

– Richard Branson

One of the most priceless lessons I carry is from my late mother, **Smt. Anita Devi**, her words still echo in my heart. She always encouraged me to try new things in life and never give up."

She believed in the magic of persistence and the beauty of exploration. That Belief became my truth.

That spirit of curiosity and resilience became my DNA.

Whenever I succeeded, I thanked her teachings.

My mentors, too, have played a critical role. As I grew older and ventured deeper into the business world, I began to understand the true meaning of **entrepreneurship.**

It's not merely about financial transactions or making money—

It's about **solving problems, adding value**, and **staying true to your roots.**

My mentors reminded me that business is not a sprint; it's a marathon fueled by vision, character, and consistency.

"Choose a job you love, and you will never have to work a day in your life."
– Confucius

This book is not a blueprint. It's a conversation.

It's me sharing what I've learned—both the sweet and the bitter—and offering it to you with complete honesty. I'm not here to preach. I'm here to connect, to inspire, and share the **LALA principles** that transformed my life and can transform yours too.

At the heart of everything I do is a simple mantra:

" Keep working on yourself because change is constant."

This book reflects the timeless wisdom passed down to me and how I applied those learnings to create my own path. No matter how experienced you are, you're always a **student of life**. Growth never stops. Learning never ends.

And for me, **work** is not a burden—it's a blessing. It's where I find meaning, joy, and identity.

- For me, work is not just an occupation: **Work is PASSION.**
- **Work is PLAY.**
- **Work is WORSHIP.**
- **Work is LIFE.**

And when you truly love what you do, growth becomes effortless and success becomes inevitable.

My Journey: Rooted in Purpose, Driven by Karma

This book is my journey — a reflection of how every person I've met, every experience I've lived, and every value I've inherited have shaped me in all aspects of life: **mental, physical, emotional**, and especially **entrepreneurial**.

While life has many dimensions, this book focuses on **my entrepreneurial evolution** — a journey not built in a boardroom, but at the **dinner table**, in crowded **train compartments**, on the **shop floor**, and most importantly, in the **company of my family.**

As the *Bhagavad Gita* says:

"Karma is not just about getting what you give — it's about becoming who you are meant to be, and attracting people that reflect your true purpose."

From my childhood, I have watched my **father and Chachaji** work tirelessly to establish themselves in business. They started young, with no comforts, no cushion — just **raw hustle and sheer *"mehnat."***

I remember them traveling for over **60 days at a stretch**, in sleeper coaches, tirelessly visiting towns, taking orders, handling dispatches, extending credit, learning new ways, and implementing what they learned on the go.

They had no formal training, no strategy decks — but what they had was **commitment, unity, and clarity of purpose.**

Their journey from **wooden packaging vendors** to **leading players in the toy industry** wasn't just inspiring; it became the blueprint for how I saw life and business.

Behind them stood the quiet strength of our family: my **grandmother**, the matriarch, the emotional compass of the house. She wasn't a businesswoman on paper, but her wisdom guided the men who were. I remember them discussing ideas at the dinner table while I listened silently. Back then, I didn't realize it, but those conversations were **my first lessons in leadership, risk, ethics, and ambition.**

Business in the Blood — Lessons from the Family

My **siblings and cousins** were no different. Business wasn't a career path for them, it was in their **blood.** Every gathering became a masterclass in identifying opportunity, negotiating smartly, and thinking two steps ahead.

They taught me early:

> "Opportunity is everything. If you don't see it, someone else will."

We were a big joint family. And in such a competitive but supportive environment, **each one of us had to push harder,** not just to survive, but to **outshine, outperform, and outgrow**.

That upbringing **sharpened my instincts.**

It made me an **opportunist** in the best sense of the word — someone who watches the game carefully, who sees the window when it opens, and who runs through it before others even notice.

I developed a fire within — a hunger to **win**, to perform, to rise, no matter what the odds.

For me, it's always been:

WIN. WIN. WIN.

Not just against others, but against yesterday's version of myself.

From Loss to Learning —
No Shortcuts in Business

"We learn from our mistakes, but never stop, and keep moving. We will definitely find a way."

I made many mistakes in my pursuit of success. But those mistakes made me stronger. Wiser. More grounded in who I am and how I choose to do business.

Let me share one of the most important — and painful — incidents of my life.

A story that became one of the biggest LALA lessons I've ever lived through.

A New Start — With Old Energy

I had just finished my graduation. Eager to prove myself, I joined our family business and was entrusted with the **accounts and automation systems**, which, back then, were still mostly manual. I put in long hours, stayed behind the scenes, and handled backend operations with quiet discipline.

But over time, I realized something important: **Sales and marketing were the real drivers of visibility and influence.** My cousins and family members who were active in those areas gained more recognition, more say, and more respect.

And I craved that.

I wanted to prove myself, to be seen, and to win my place at the table.

A Shortcut That Turned into a Setback

Motivated by that ambition, I joined hands with a **childhood friend** to start a new business, something I believed would give me a "shortcut" to success and stature.

But instead of a partner, I became a **silent passenger.** He used my money, but never involved me in real decision-making. I thought I was building something, but I was just **being used.**

No meaningful learning.

No growth.

Only **losses** — financially, emotionally, and personally.

Eventually, the business collapsed.

I lost the money I had invested.

More painfully, I lost a **childhood friendship** that had spanned years.

And perhaps hardest of all, I faced disappointment in the eyes of my family.

I felt like I had failed them.

The Real Lesson

That moment could have broken me.

But I turned to the LALA Principles I had grown up hearing - at the dinner table, in family meetings, in whispered wisdom from elders.

Shortcuts are never the way to success.

Only hard work, learning, and wise decision-making bring real growth.

Yes, I made a mistake.

Yes, I paid a price.

But I bounced back.

Because mistakes are not the end — they are part of the path. They teach us where to walk, where not to trust, **and how to rise stronger.**

What I Learned:

- Don't run from the back seat to the driver's seat without knowing the road.
- Friendship and business need boundaries and clarity.
- There is no replacement for experience and wisdom.
- You can lose money, but never lose your self-worth.
- True respect comes from substance, not shortcuts.

Even today, I believe in giving **credit,** in **trust,** and in **taking calculated risks** — but now with far more awareness and control.

You don't fail because you made a mistake.

You only fail if you don't learn from it.

And if you're living the LALA Way:

Then every mistake… is just **another step toward mastery**

Now that you have peeked into my journey, are you ready to embark on a journey that will elevate & enhance your entrepreneurial mindset, sharpen your business instincts, fuel your drive, and unlock the entrepreneur within you?

Let's walk this path together—with **curiosity, humility, energy,** and **a whole lot of heart.**

Let's BEGIN with a **smile, with love,** and with a mind ready to grow.

Here we go!

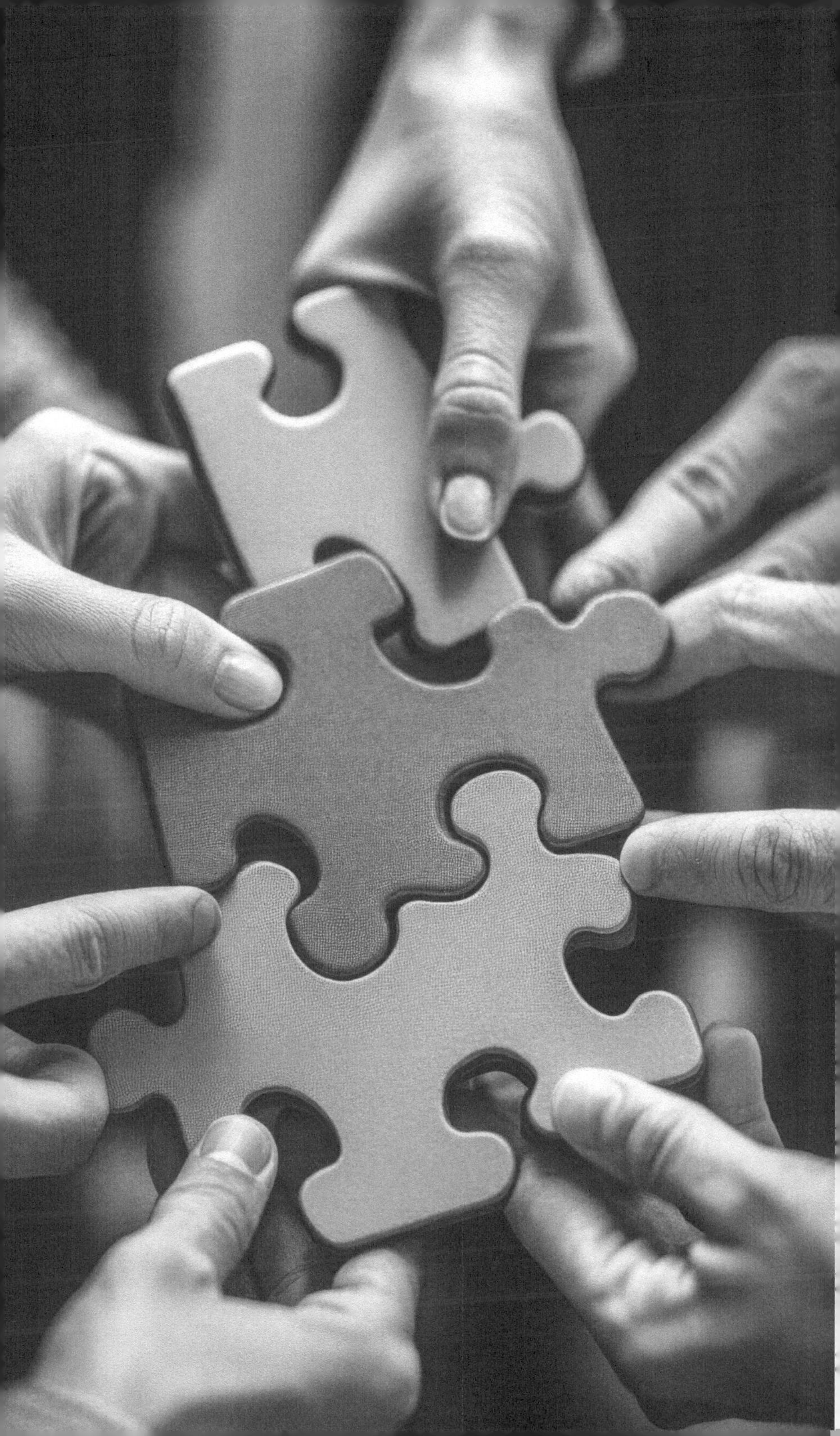

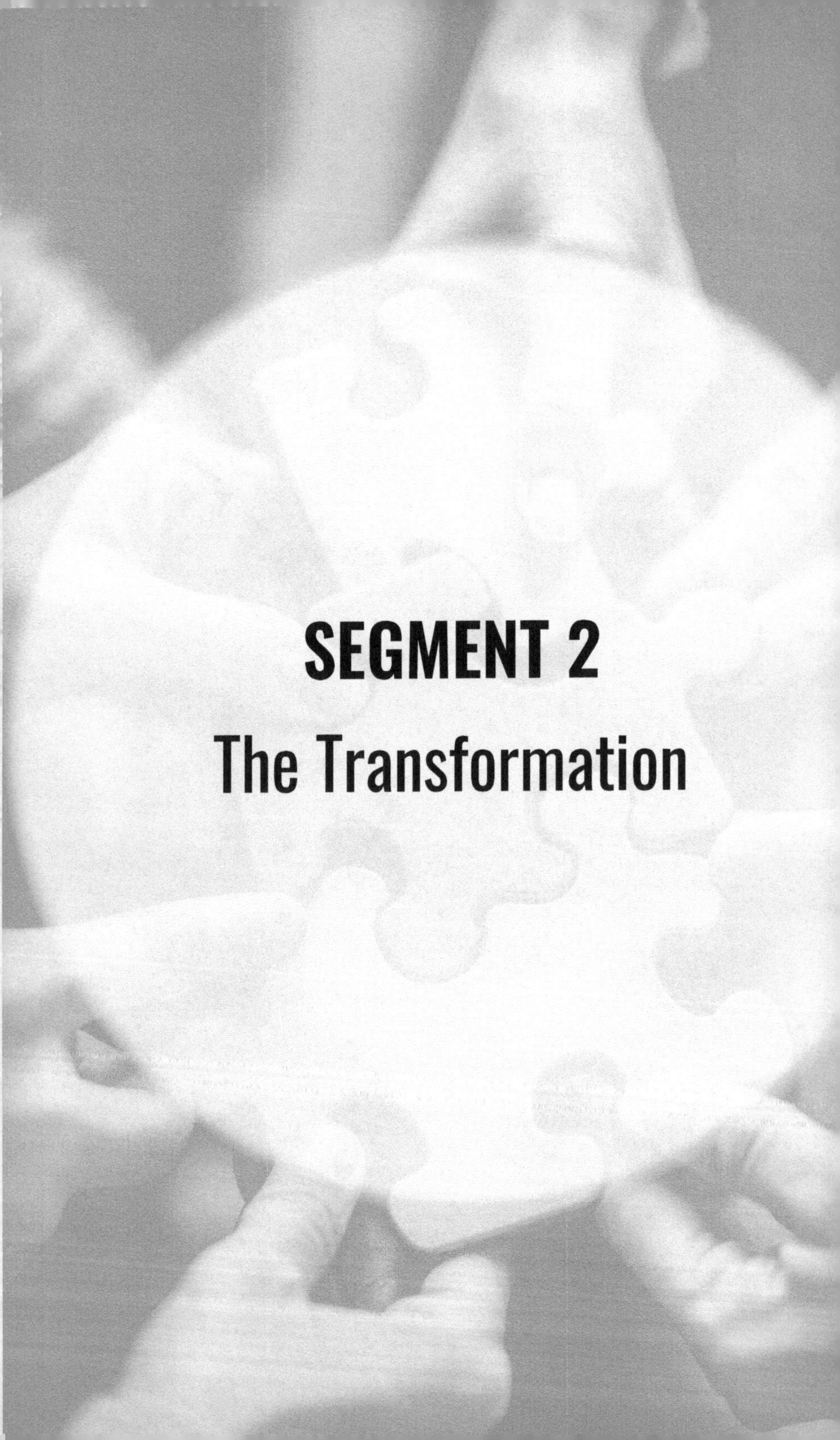

SEGMENT 2

The Transformation

After laying a strong foundation of timeless values and business ethics, Segment 2: The Transformation marks a powerful shift from understanding to living it. This section is all about evolving your mindset.

In today's fast-changing world, it's not enough to hold good values; we must learn how to live, apply, and lead with them.

This segment shows how everyday discipline, long-term thinking, commitment to promises, and respect for every relationship can actually transform your life and business from the inside out.

It's not about big capital or degrees, it's about building credibility, staying adaptable, and showing up with integrity, day after day.

Here you'll find deeply personal, relatable stories and practical wisdom on:

➢ The power of words, promises, and delivery.

➢ Why loyalty to your business comes before luxury.

➢ Why the customer is not just king, but God.

➢ The real impact of financial discipline, structure, and intention.

➢ And how small, consistent actions build empires over time.

This segment is a toolkit for inner change, because before your business grows, you must grow, and for growth, you must.

➢ **CHANGE Your Mind-set**: Always embrace everything with a smile & fun Hurdles & hardships are just temporary; face them, frame them, and move on!

➢ **BELIEVE in Yourself**: Your belief is your foundation, and continuous effort will be the key to success.

- **Have a Clear VISION!:** If your vision is clear, then even reaching the **Moon or Mars** is achievable. I **learned from My Mentors that "Vision gives direction to life."**

In the following pages, I share with you the principles that guided my journey and continue to inspire me daily.

If Segment 1 was your awakening, Segment 2 is your evolution.

Let's begin the transformation.....

CHAPTER 4

The Power of Words and Commitment

Your word is your worth. Once broken, it's hard to rebuild."

Let me share the most important lesson I have learned from my LALA PRINCIPLES

In the world I grew up in, **a person's word was their bond.**

There were no legal contracts—just verbal promises, sealed with a handshake and an unwavering commitment to deliver.

My father once told me,

"A businessman's biggest asset is his credibility. If people trust your word, you'll never be out of business."

Your **words hold the greatest value in life.** If a promise is made, it must be fulfilled.

This principle came alive when I started my own entrepreneurial journey. There were moments when I could have taken the easier route, backed out of a deal, or shifted blame. But I remembered those lessons.

Keeping my word, even when it was inconvenient, paid off in the long run. People began to see me as dependable. And in business, that's gold.

I want to share an experience that deeply touched me and strengthened my belief in the power of words & commitment as not just words but as an action.

I have always believed the true essence of business lies in keeping your promises, no matter how big the challenges you face.

During my childhood, when I must have been 9 years old, I learned about the importance of keeping promises. My father taught me this lesson that I still hold in my heart.

Commitment is an Act: Not Just a Word!

One Diwali, while I was playing with firecrackers. One firecracker that I lit accidentally set my neighbour's house on fire. Their entire house burned down, and when the neighbours found out that I was responsible for their loss, they came to my father, complaining, and he committed that if my son is the cause of your distress, I will compensate for your loss.

My father could have avoided the situation by saying, **"He is just a child, why should I compensate for the loss?"** But instead, he stood by his word and took full responsibility. He firmly told them, **"My son did it, and I will do whatever it takes to make it right."**

Though that decision was a difficult financial one.

Still to keep his word, my father sold valuables, including my mother's jewellery, and even took a loan to compensate for their loss.

This cemented our family reputation & faith in us, our neighbours still respect my family and always speak about the act of words and commitment. This experience made me strong and instilled **unshakable confidence in always doing the right thing.** It taught me that, no matter how difficult the circumstances, one must always **honour their word and stay committed**...

"Commitment is an act, not a word."

My father's action embodied this.

CHAPTER 5

The Value of Timely Delivery & Honoured Promises

"Good intentions are meaningless if you don't deliver on your promise."

In the LALA principles learned since my childhood, I have seen that if someone commits something, it becomes a statement to honour, and even if it is not contracted, we honour it as if it were legally binding.

" *Jabaan ki keemat*" *(The Value of Words)* is an act to be honoured!

In business, one **critical application of this principle is timely delivery. Honouring your commitment by sticking to your promised delivery schedule shows professionalism, builds reputation, and reflects respect for others' time.**

"Punctuality is not merely about being on time. It's about respecting your own commitments. "

Promises are made to let the other person know that we are confident about what we are saying, and you can rest assured.

Let me share a personal story about **timely delivery.**

Praan Jaaye Par Vachan Na Jaaye: Promises are Dearer Than Life!

Once we accepted a **large order from a big customer** with an extremely tight delivery timeline. However, because our commitment meant the world to us, we made it a point to **fulfill our promise on time.**

My entire team worked tirelessly, **day and night**, to meet the deadline.

Such was the culture of commitment and honouring promises in our company that even my staff's wives and their families worked alongside us unconditionally; this was not something that I asked them to do, they got them along voluntarily, knowing the value of honouring promises and timely delivery.

This ensured that every detail was taken care of.

Of course, despite all the challenges, we delivered on time, as promised.

That **on-time delivery** became a turning point in my journey.

Today, I am among the top vendors for that customer, and this experience reinforced my belief that:

- **Timely delivery always pays off!**
- **One should always strive to keep promises!**

CHAPTER 6

Loyalty to Business, Pay First, Spend Later – The Key to Prosperity

"Treat your business like a child—nurture it, protect it, and it will grow with you."

The first L in the LALA Principles stands for Loyalty — not to a person or trend, but to the business itself.

Business is like a living being. It needs your attention, protection, and nourishment. A true LALA never takes the business for granted. They know every penny, every transaction, and every customer matters.

During tough times, I've seen Baniya shopkeepers cut down their personal expenses but never compromise on reinvesting in their shops. That's loyalty—putting the business first.

This principle guided me when my startup hit a rough patch. While others looked for exits, I doubled down. I was loyal to the mission, the team, and the customers. Eventually, that persistence paid off.

We had a clear course of action; we were determined to clear all outstanding first, and then only did we intend to spend on ourselves, so that we wouldn't be under any pressure and would be free from our liability. Though it is an ongoing process of business, we still try to clear the market outstanding beforehand. It makes our reputation in the market rock solid.

Let me share an experience that shaped my financial discipline.

The Difficult Path is Often Profitable!

We were two friends who started out our businesses at nearly the same time, but our **upbringings** and financial habits were completely different.

- I always believed in **clearing payments first**, even when credit was available. I utilized **cash discounts** and prioritized clearing **market dues** before spending on personal luxuries.
- On the other hand, my friend had a different approach—**he took loans to meet the business requirement and spent all his profits lavishly on a luxurious lifestyle.**

At one point, people questioned my choices. They said, **"Why are you paying the market first? You could use that money more wisely and live better."**

However, I stayed grounded and followed my **principles.**

Over time, the wisdom of my difficult and disciplined choices was clear for all to see.

My friend drowned in debt and eventually went bankrupt due to lavish spending and not realising the aftereffects. However, despite many challenges, my business not only sustained itself but thrived.

The market always observes how we handle trade, and my real-life experience reinforced this:

- **Pay first, spend later.**
- **Clear market dues before indulging in luxuries.**
- **Financial discipline is the foundation of long-term success.**

Use your funds like a debit card and don't become a credit card; enjoy first and pay later.

Financial discipline is the backbone of a sustainable business. When you pay first and manage your expenses later, you avoid debt traps and keep control over your growth..

CHAPTER 7

Customer is Not Just King, Customer is God

> ***"Respect is the soil in which lasting relationships grow."***

A customer brings you business, feedback, and referrals. Treat them like God, not out of fear, but out of gratitude. Respect is a currency that pays the highest returns.

> "If you don't genuinely value your customer, someone else will."

Respect isn't commanded—it's earned, both in life and in business. In our community, respect is shown by how you treat others, especially those who work for you.

My grandfather ran a small shop. Every morning, before opening the shutters, he would touch the floor and offer a small prayer—not just to the deities but to the business itself. He respected the trade, the customers, and the staff. That humility earned him immense goodwill.

When I launched my office, I tried to bring the same respect into our culture, respecting employees, customers, and even competitors. It created a space of mutual growth. People are more likely to collaborate, support, and even forgive when there's genuine respect.

I firmly believe in this LALA principle. I want to share an interesting story of mine that highlights the power of **Respect and LOVE** in business.

People Never Forget How You Treat Them!

There was once a **low-profile buyer** whom many in the market **did not take seriously**. People judged him based on his background and **did not consider him worthy of trust**. Many traders refused to prioritize his orders, assuming he wasn't reliable.

However, I always believed in **respecting every customer and fulfilling their commitments, no matter their status**. We always honoured his orders and treated him with **the same dedication** as any other high-profile client.

Years later, this buyer **rose to the top of the industry,** becoming one of the biggest entities in his field. Since we had **respected and supported him in his early days,** he continued to **respect and support** us as he grew in status.

This experience taught me a powerful lesson:

- Never judge a customer based on their current status.
- Trust, respect, and dedication always come back in unexpected ways.
- Rapport and relationships are the real wealth in business.

CHAPTER 8

Deliver More Than You Promise

"Always exceed your customers' expectations. Surprise them with more." – Sam Walton

Going the extra mile doesn't just surprise your customer—it secures their loyalty. Under-promise, over-deliver. That's the secret to standing out in a crowded market.

Let me share my personal experience :

A very simple yet powerful tool to convert a partial sales order into a total ORDER.

Once, we negotiated with a buyer on a price point and finalized a deal. However, after revisiting the product, we realized that with minor adjustments, we could add two extra features at the same cost.

Instead of increasing our profit and being satisfied with the deal, we chose to enhance the product quality and deliver more than what was promised.

The Result?

That additional feature converted a 30 percent regular order into a total ORDER and strengthened our business ethics.

The Lesson

Over-delivering builds trust, credibility, and long-term success.

CHAPTER 9

Betrayal is The Worst Sin

> ***"It takes 20 years to build a reputation and five minutes to ruin it." Warren Buffet***

In business, nothing is more fragile or more powerful than trust.

You can lose money and recover. But lose your reputation, and you lose everything.

In the traditional Baniya ethos, the idea of betrayal — of a customer, partner, or vendor is not just unethical, it's unthinkable.

We are taught from childhood: **"Bharosa todna paap hai."** (Breaking trust is a sin.)

Shortcuts built on lies, manipulations, or backstabbing may offer quick gains. But they never build lasting businesses. I've seen traders who manipulated weights or mixed lower-quality goods into shipments. They made some profit once. But within months, word spread. Their phones stopped ringing, their shelves started gathering dust.

On the other hand, I remember a time when a supplier accidentally sent us extra stock, high-value items.

My team debated: "Should we keep it? They might not even notice."

However, we returned it the same day. The supplier was stunned.

From that day onward, he offered us better margins and exclusive access to new product lines, simply because he trusted us like family.

Even in tough times, integrity must remain non-negotiable. One wrong invoice, one bad deal, one betrayal, and years of goodwill can vanish overnight.

So remember:

Your brand isn't your logo or product — it's your name.

Guard it like a crown. Clean money is slow, but it's sustainable. Dirty tricks may feel smart until they destroy everything.

In the end, business is not about outsmarting others. It's about outlasting, and you only outlast when you are trusted.

Many businesses follow the market trend of **cutting product sizes** to save costs. Customers may not immediately notice, but this **compromises integrity.**

We chose a different path.

We always provided **full-size, quality products** instead of **deceiving customers with reduced sizes.**

Because of this **honest approach**, our **brand earned fame and reliability** in the market. Customers trust us, and our business continues to flourish.

The Lesson

Integrity builds lasting businesses. Betrayal may bring short-term profits, but honesty ensures long-term success.

"When you betray somebody else, you also betray yourself."

CHAPTER 10

Buy Cash, Sell Credit – The Ultimate Trade Formula

"Cash flow is the lifeblood of any business. Protect it like your life depends on it — because it does."

In our Indian marketplace, this formula has quietly powered traders and shopkeepers for generations:

"Cash mein kharido, udhaar mein becho."

(Buy in cash, sell on credit.)

It may sound simple, but this is a strategic play — one that builds financial discipline, trust, and long-term leverage.

When you buy in cash, you gain three key advantages:

1. **Better rates:** Sellers love certainty. Cash gets you discounts.
2. **No liabilities:** No interest, no late penalties.
3. **Respect:** Vendors take you seriously when you pay upfront.

Cash Is King!

I still remember visiting a wholesaler in Sadar Bazaar in my early days. I walked in with cash while most others requested 15-30 day terms.

He gave me a better rate without me even asking, and priority during peak season.

That relationship, built on cash respect, lasted years.

Credit Is A Privilege!

On the selling side, offering short-term credit to good customers helps you build loyalty and volume. But here's the catch — it must be **disciplined** and well-tracked.

Not everyone deserves credit. It's a tool, not a default.

We once had a new distributor who requested a 60-day cycle. We checked his background, reputation, and payment history. After cautious trials and prompt payments, we extended it. He felt trusted and began pushing our products harder than anyone else.

However, we also learned the hard way. A client we trusted delayed payments repeatedly, causing a cash crunch. After two strikes, we shifted them back to advance terms.

Credit is a privilege, not a right.

This formula—**buying cash and selling on credit**- keeps the business running like a well-oiled machine. You preserve liquidity on one end and nurture growth on the other.

Modern startups often forget this. They chase scale and sacrifice solvency. But a seasoned Lala knows, **revenue is vanity, cash flow is sanity.**

Because of this policy, everyone in the trade wants to work with us. Our name has become a brand when it comes to payments and credibility.

- We give **suppliers confidence with upfront cash payments.**
- In return, we **always receive the best price and fastest deliveries** from factories.

The Lesson

Financial discipline and credibility are key to sustainable business growth.

CHAPTER 11

Customise Business Terms for Customers

"To serve each customer uniquely is to build a business universally admired."

Rules are important. But rigid rules, when applied without wisdom, can damage relationships.

In the Baniya mindset, nazaakat— the finesse to adapt without compromising values is a treasured skill.

Flexibility is not about being inconsistent; it's about understanding the bigger picture. It's about knowing when to bend so the relationship doesn't break.

Let me share a story.

The Rigid Fall, The Flexible Thrive

A loyal client, who had always paid on time and placed regular orders, once asked for an extended credit period during an industry slowdown. By policy, we were strict about payment cycles, 30 days, no exceptions. My team was hesitant.

But I knew this customer. He was trustworthy. I called him personally, listened, and offered a 45-day window. He was relieved and promised to return the favor when things stabilized.

And he did.

Not only did he repay before time, but in the months that followed, he doubled his business with us and brought in two new clients, just because we stood by him when he needed it.

Another time, a retailer in a small town had trouble meeting our minimum order quantity.

Instead of refusing the deal, we adjusted the MOQ slightly and included a mix of fast-moving products to support him.

That store now displays our products in their prime shelf space — by choice, not negotiation.

These are not exceptions. These are *investments in trust.*

Flexibility builds reputation. It shows that you don't just follow policy, you understand people. And in the long game of business, that understanding is your real differentiator.

The world remembers fairness. But it deeply respects empathy.

According to **The Lala Principle**, business is about:

- Understanding/studying **systems and operations, customer cycle, and requirements** to provide them with **the best facilities.**
- **Analysing their needs** and fulfilling them **efficiently.**

The Lesson

Flexibility in business leads to customer satisfaction and long-term relationships.

CHAPTER 12

Value Everyone

> ***"Treat everyone with politeness, even those who are rude to you — not because they are nice, but because you are."***

This Lala principle makes you realise that every person, no matter how small their role, adds value.

A strong business is not built only by visionaries, strategists, or salespeople. It's built by those who sweep the floor before anyone arrives, those who enter bills into dusty ledgers, those who answer calls patiently all day, and those who lock up after everyone has left.

In the Baniya tradition, we are taught to see value in everyone, not just because of what they do, but because of who we are.

Little Acts Lead To Snowball Effects

I'll never forget an incident from our early years. A young boy worked in our warehouse, barely 18, quiet, often overlooked. One day, during a particularly hectic dispatch, he noticed that a box had been mislabeled and loaded with the wrong items. He quietly brought it to our attention before it left.

That simple act saved us from a major client embarrassment and potential loss.

We thanked him publicly, gave him a small bonus, but more importantly, we gave him a voice in our daily meetings. Years later, he became one of our most dependable logistics managers.

All because someone chose to value his contribution early on.

Another time, a visiting client was about to walk in. Our office boy, Ramesh, who had been with us for years, noticed the water glasses on the meeting table were smudged. Without being told, he replaced them and wiped the table clean. The client later remarked, "You can tell a lot about a company by how they treat their office staff — and how the staff responds in return."

That hit me deeply.

In the fast-moving business world, titles and designations can often blind us. But I've seen again and again that loyalty and excellence come not just from managers with degrees, but from peons, clerks, helpers, drivers, and guards who feel respected.

Valuing everyone isn't just good leadership, it's good business. People who feel seen serve better. They speak up, take ownership, and protect the business like it's their own.

True power lies in kindness. And the strongest leaders are the ones who never forget this.

CHAPTER 13

Always Learn and Expand Your Capabilities

> ***"The illiterate of the 21st century are not those who can't read or write, but those who can't learn, unlearn, and relearn."***
>
> ***– Alvin Toffler***

This principle is more than advice, it's a **blessing** passed down from my elders and one of the most foundational LALA Principles in my journey. From my childhood, I've been encouraged to constantly seek knowledge, sharpen my skills, and stay hungry to grow.

In the old days, my **Chacha ji** would finish his accounts, close the shop, and spend an hour walking through the market, not to buy or sell, but to observe.

- What are others doing?
- Which product is moving fast?
- What are customers asking for?

That curiosity, that hunger to learn, is what kept him sharp and respected in the entire market.

Today, the market has changed. It's no longer just about physical footfall or margins, **it's about digital reach, customer psychology, new tools, and shifting consumer trends.**

The rules have evolved, but the core principle remains the same:

"The one who learns the fastest, adapts the quickest."

I've made it a personal habit to invest at least **30 minutes a day** in learning, whether it's:

- Reading an insightful article
- Watching a short business video
- Talking to someone younger or more experienced
- Reflecting quietly on the day's wins and losses

Lifelong Learning: The Key To Success

Some of my best ideas didn't come from boardroom meetings. They came from listening to a delivery boy, a customer complaint, or a junior staff member with a fresh perspective.

Once, a young intern suggested we use **WhatsApp for B2B order confirmations**. At first, I laughed — "That's too casual!" I said. But we tried it.

Within weeks, order response time dropped by 50%. That one suggestion became a permanent system.

Another time, during a business slowdown, I enrolled in an online digital **marketing course.** Sitting in a virtual class with college students felt strange, even humbling. But that knowledge helped us reinvent our marketing strategy during COVID, reaching new customers when many competitors were stuck.

Inspired by these learnings, I began **exploring new verticals, attending learning forums, and reading more books** than ever before. Within three months, I saw a visible transformation in my:

- Business mindset
- Personal growth
- Even physical health

It was like seeing a "before and after" version of myself — more confident, more focused, and more resilient.

So I tell every young entrepreneur this:

- Don't wait for opportunities. Prepare yourself for them.
- Don't fear what you don't know. Learn it.
- Because in today's world, **knowledge is compound interest**, the more you invest, the more you grow.

The Lesson

Continuous learning is not just a habit — it's a multiplier.

CHAPTER 14

Never Judge a Customer by their Looks

"Every customer carries potential — but not all of them wear it on their sleeves."

"Har grahak mein bhagwan basta hai — par har bhagwan kurta-pyjama mein nahi aata."

This is one of the most underrated and powerful LALA Principles — **never judge a customer by appearance.**

- Don't confuse simplicity with lack of worth.
- Don't confuse flashiness with real business.

A seasoned businessman learns to look beyond clothes, language, or demeanor. He pays attention to **intent, consistency, and curiosity.**

I've seen clients walk into shops in sandals and faded shirts — and place orders worth lakhs.

I've also seen customers in luxury cars bargain for hours and disappear without buying anything.

I remember one day, a quiet man came to our warehouse. He looked like a small-town trader, very modest in dressing, no business card, no entourage. Some of our staff didn't give him much attention. But I sat with him, offered tea, and listened. He asked deep questions about the product, took notes, and said he was trying something new in his town.

A week later, he placed a small order. Then a bigger one. Within months, he was one of our largest rural distributors.

His only feedback: *"You treated me like I mattered, when no one else did."*

It was a powerful lesson.

Business is not about impressing customers— it's about valuing them.

Look at:

- How interested they are in the product
- What kind of questions do they ask
- How seriously they discuss logistics, service, and repeat orders

That will tell you who they are, not their attire or accent.

This principle has paid us again and again, in loyalty, in scale, and in surprises.

So next time someone walks in who doesn't "look the part," offer them the same respect, service, and attention. **In business, you're not dealing with appearances — you're dealing with potential.**

CHAPTER 15

Hard Work Always Pays – and Gives Joy

"Be the master, not just of skills, but of effort."

This is one of the most cherished LALA Principles I've learned from my elders, and lived in my own journey: **Hard work always pays. And more than that, it gives joy.**

Growing up, I saw a culture where no one waited for reminders or alarms. My **elders would begin their day at 9 AM sharp**, sometimes earlier, not because they were told to, but **because they were driven.** I'd often see my father sitting at the desk with his tea, calmly writing in the ledger as the city still yawned into its day.

That quiet discipline, repeated daily, left a deep impression on me.

They didn't believe in wasting time — and they certainly didn't believe that **"smart shortcuts" could replace sincere effort.**

"Kaam mein maza tabhi aata hai jab dil se kiya jaye."

My grandfather used to say, "Work becomes joy when done with the heart, not just the hands."

In today's world, everyone talks about ***smart work.***

Yes, working efficiently matters. **But without hard work as your foundation, smartness has no direction.**

It's like trying to sail without wind.

I remember in our early days, we couldn't afford many staff. I used to **load trucks, write invoices, and make follow-up calls** myself. My shirt would be soaked, my legs would ache, but my heart was full — because I knew we were building something. Brick by brick. Load by load.

And that labor taught me things no MBA ever could:

- The importance of detail
- The patience to solve problems
- The pride of doing something with your own hands

> "Smart work may win a battle, but hard work wins the war."

As the business grew, I didn't stop working hard — I just worked smarter *because* I had earned the right through sweat.

So here's the truth:

- There are no shortcuts to mastery
- There's no substitute for effort
- And there's joy in the grind — if you do it with purpose

The Lesson

The Lala doesn't shy away from labor. He embraces it. Because hard work is not just about income — it's about identity.

Become the master, not just of a business, but of your own effort and integrity.

CHAPTER 16

Never Say "No" to a Customer – Always Try to Arrange It

"A Lala doesn't reject — he finds a way."

This principle has been a **pillar of my success**, not just in business, but in how I've built relationships that have lasted years, sometimes generations.

In the traditional marketplace, customers return not just because of price or product, but because they **feel heard.** And more importantly, **they feel served.**

One of the best things I learned early on was this:

Don't say "No" — say "Let me try."

I remember a loyal client once called, asking for a specific product we didn't usually stock. The easy route was to say, "Sorry, we don't keep that." But instead, I picked up the phone, called a few vendors, and made some arrangements.

It took a bit of extra effort. But the customer never forgot it. He said, ***"You didn't have it, but you made it happen. That's what I value."***

That client went on to refer two others to us. And all of them stayed because they trusted not just our catalog, they trusted our commitment to find solutions.

Of course, we can't say yes to every impossible request. But even the willingness to try tells the customer that they matter.

It tells them:

"We're not here just to sell. We're here to serve."

If we truly **understand our customers' needs**

If we **build a strong internal system**

If we **earn their trust consistently...**

They will never leave us.

"Customers don't stay because you're convenient — they stay because you're dependable."

The Lesson

Saying "Yes" to a customer's need — or at least trying to — creates relationships that no advertisement ever can. It's not just about selling products. It's about **building loyalty with effort.**

> **In business, always be known as the person who "figures it out."**
> **That reputation is priceless.**

CHAPTER 17

Always Ask Your Customer What They Need — and Provide It

> ***"If you listen to your customer, they will give you the roadmap to success."***

In business, one of the most dangerous things we can do is **assume**:

- ➢ Assume we know what the customer wants.
- ➢ Assume what worked yesterday will work today.
- ➢ Assume that if we talk more, we'll sell more.

The truth? Listening is the real superpower.

Time and again, I've seen product launches fail — not because the product was bad, but because the business owner created what *they* liked instead of what the **market needed.**

Meanwhile, businesses that truly listen grow quietly but consistently — because they align with real demand, not imagined preferences.

One of my favorite practices, taught to me by my father, was simple yet powerful:

Ask every customer at least one question.

- "What are you looking for that you're not finding?"
- "Is there anything we can do better?"
- "What's missing in your store that your customers keep asking about?".

During a business slowdown, I visited retailers personally.

I didn't pitch. I simply listened.

One shopkeeper said,

"Customers are asking for smaller packs. ₹100 is too much right now — ₹30 feels easier."

That one line changed everything.

We launched mini-packs, adjusted pricing, and within weeks, our sales surged in Tier 2 and Tier 3 towns.

The market was talking. We just had to shut up and listen.

Another time, a corporate client casually mentioned they struggled to track their bulk orders.

So we created a simple Excel order tracker just for them — not part of our service, but it solved a real pain point.

That small gesture built more loyalty than any fancy discount ever could.

Because customers don't expect perfection — **They expect understanding.**

The Lesson

If you truly listen, your customer will sell your product back to you, with insights you'd never imagine.

You'll stop pushing sales.

They'll start pulling your business forward.

> Never guess what your customers want.
> Ask. And deliver.
> That's how you earn business — and keep it.

CHAPTER 18

Relationship First, Profit and Loss Later

> ***"Business is about relationships. The rest is just numbers."***

In today's fast-paced world, everything is measured in ROI, margins, and quarterly growth. But in the traditional Baniya mindset, and my own journey, I've learned this powerful truth:

Profit comes and goes. But relationships last and compound.

I've always believed that the real capital in business is trust, not just turnover. Numbers fluctuate. Markets shift. But genuine bonds? They open doors you didn't even know existed.

Let me share a personal example.

Years ago, we had a vendor who had consistently delivered for us. One season, due to his own supply chain issues, he delayed a major shipment. We suffered losses — we had to refund clients and even bear a few penalties.

My team was frustrated and wanted to blacklist him immediately.

But I remembered all the times he had prioritized us, even worked overtime to help us meet impossible timelines.

So instead of cutting him off, I called him and said: *"I know this season hurt, but our relationship matters more than one bad deal."*

He was shocked — and deeply moved.

The very next season, he went out of his way to help us during our biggest Diwali push.

He gave us better rates

Exclusive stock

And even helped finance part of the inventory.

That single gesture of grace created a partnership that lasted over a decade.

Another time, we had a long-time client who defaulted on a payment, a significant amount. Everyone advised me to go legal or cut ties. But I knew his character, and I knew his situation. We offered him a flexible payment plan and gave him space.

He cleared every rupee, with interest. And he stayed loyal for years after, referring high-value clients to us as a token of gratitude.

> "Sometimes, the bond you build during someone's weakest moment becomes your strongest asset."

In business, we often obsess over balance sheets. But it's the **emotional ledger** — of how you treat people — that truly decides your long-term success.

Relationships may not show up in quarterly reports. But they **build brand equity** that no advertisement ever can.

The Lesson

Never let short-term profit blind you to long-term loyalty.

Trust, once earned, is worth more than any invoice.

> In business, as in life, **relationships are the only currency that appreciates with time.**

CHAPTER 19

Positive Intention Always Gives Positive Results

"Energy flows where intention goes."

In the world of business, we often talk about planning, marketing, sales, and strategy.

But behind all of it lies something more powerful — your intention.

When your intention is clear, honest, and positive — when your heart is in the right place — the business aligns in mysterious, meaningful ways. Customers feel it. Partners trust it. Even the challenges that come your way start to feel like stepping stones instead of roadblocks.

In the LALA way of doing business, we call this

"Neeyat Saaf toh Safalta Pakki"

— Pure intent guarantees eventual success.

Let me share a story that proved this to me.

A few years ago, we launched a small side project — a new product line that wasn't our core offering. We didn't expect much from it. The margins were low, and there was no aggressive sales plan behind it.

But the intention was different.

The idea was born after a customer mentioned how difficult it was to find **affordable, good-quality products for rural markets**. We listened. And though it wasn't a highly profitable move, we built the product anyway, keeping **quality intact** and **pricing sensitive**.

When we launched, it moved slowly. But we stayed consistent — because our intention was never to make a quick buck.

It was to solve a real problem.

Within six months, word-of-mouth began spreading. Retailers from other towns started calling. Distributors reached out asking if we had plans for new variants. What started as a small, purpose-driven initiative quietly became a **growth engine** — and today, it's one of our most respected product lines.

Why did it work?

Because it was born from a place of **service, not strategy**. And people can sense that.

Another time, a client was unhappy with a batch, though the issue wasn't directly our fault. Instead of arguing or deflecting blame, we replaced the full order at our cost.

That single gesture, made with the intention to maintain trust, turned the client into a lifelong advocate.

He later told me, *"I work with many vendors, but very few care like you do. That's why I stick with you."*

It reminded me: **It's not just the product — it's the *energy* behind the product.**

The Lesson

- When your **intent is to help, not just to sell…**
- When your **focus is on value, not just volume…**
- When your **energy is positive, and your actions are consistent...**

Success follows — sometimes slowly, but always surely.

In business, your *intentions set the vibration.* And vibration creates reality.

So every morning, before you check your stock or sales, **check your *neeyat.***

That's what truly drives growth — in your work, and in your life.

CHAPTER 20

Constantly Innovating

"Innovate or die." – Peter Drucker

In the Baniya tradition, we deeply value consistency, but we're not afraid of change.

Because while values stay the same, **methods must evolve.**

- What worked yesterday may not work tomorrow.
- Your bestselling product might slow down.
- Your most efficient system might turn outdated.
- Your reliable team might need new tools to grow.

That's why innovation is not just about inventing something new, **it's about improving what you already do.**

The smartest LALAS I've known don't just innovate products, they innovate:

- **Processes** (How can we do this faster, cheaper, smoother?)
- **Systems** (Can technology help reduce dependency?)
- **Customer experience** (How can we make people feel even more valued?)

Let me share a story.

We used to rely entirely on phone calls and handwritten registers to track dealer orders. It was slow, error-prone, and difficult to scale. But this was the system we knew — and it had "worked" for years.

One day, a junior team member suggested trying a **Google Form** to collect orders, with an automatic Excel backend. At first, it felt too "high-tech" for our traditional setup. But we gave it a shot with one distributor region.

To our surprise:

- Orders became clearer
- Mistakes dropped by 90%
- Follow-ups became easier

What started as a small trial became a full system within 2 months. **Innovation didn't come from a consultant — it came from being open.**

Another example

We noticed that customer complaints about packaging damage were increasing. Instead of blaming the courier or accepting it as a cost of business, we redesigned the boxes with **extra edge protection**, added **fragile labels**, and even created a short **instruction card** inside the parcel.

Guess what?

- Complaints dropped by over 70%.
- And more importantly, **customer satisfaction increased.**

We didn't create a new product.

We just innovated around the product.

The Lesson

Innovation isn't just a tech startup buzzword. It's a mindset, and a *LALA who innovates, leads.*

Ask yourself regularly:

- What can we do better than yesterday?
- Where are our leaks?
- What would our customer love that we haven't offered yet?

Even small tweaks can create big results.

> **In the LALA mindset, innovation is not rebellion, it's evolution.**
>
> It's how traditions stay alive in changing markets.
>
> So don't just protect what you've built.
>
> **Upgrade it. Evolve it. Innovate it.**

CHAPTER 21

Initiate, Innovate, and Execute

> ***"Vision without execution is hallucination."***
>
> ***– Thomas Edison***

Ideas are everywhere.

Talk is easy.

PowerPoint presentations are impressive.

But what separates a dreamer from a **doer**, a thinker from a **LALA,** is **execution.**

In my journey, I've met countless people with brilliant ideas:

- "We should launch this new line."
- "This strategy can double sales."
- "There's a market gap here, we should enter it."

And yet, most of them are still *talking* about it.

What I've learned from my elders and lived through my own business experiences is simple but profound:

Initiate. Innovate. And most importantly — Execute.

1. **Initiate: Be the one who starts.**

   In a Baniya household, we are taught early: "*Jo kaam sochta hai, woh aadha jeet chuka hota hai. Jo shuru karta hai, woh baaki aadha jeet leta hai.*"

("He who thinks through a task is already halfway there. He who starts it, wins the rest.")

I remember wanting to open a new retail vertical, but I kept waiting for the "perfect" time. One day, my uncle said something that stuck with me:

"Perfect time doesn't exist. The clock only starts when you do."

We launched with limited stock, one city, and a lean setup. It wasn't perfect, but we began. And that beginning taught us more than any research ever could.

2. **Innovate: Don't just repeat, improve.**

   As soon as we began, feedback started coming in. Some packaging wasn't working, pricing needed adjustment, and marketing had gaps. Instead of getting discouraged, we **adapted fast.**

   We updated the product line, built stronger backend processes, and adjusted the pitch. That agility made the project profitable within six months.

   Innovation is not just creating something new — it's about **evolving what you've started.**

3. **Execute: Finish strong.**

   Most people start with energy, but few finish with discipline. Execution is about **showing up daily**, especially when the excitement fades. It's about following through on commitments, timelines, and promises.

   In our Diwali season rush, I once personally supervised shipments late into the night, because a few boxes had gone missing. No one else would have noticed. But I knew that one missed promise could undo weeks of preparation.

The customer received their order, complete and on time. That year, they doubled their order.

Execution builds your reputation. And in business, reputation is everything.

The Lesson

- Everyone has ideas.
- A few get started.
- But the rare few who **start, adapt,** and **finish** become leaders.

In the LALA way, we don't just sit and dream — **we initiate, innovate, and execute.**

Because at the end of the day, action beats theory. Always.

CHAPTER 22

Build Structure, Drive Success

> ***"You do not rise to the level of your goals, you fall to the level of your systems."***
> ***– James Clear***

Many businesses begin with talent, passion, and a dream. But without a **structure**, that passion burns out. Without a **system**, that dream becomes chaos.

This *LALA Principle* has been a defining realization in my journey:

You don't grow by effort alone, you grow when effort meets process.

Structure allows you to

- Scale without losing control
- Deliver consistent quality
- Train others to run what you've built
- Reduce dependency on individuals
- Maintain sanity in busy seasons

Let me share a moment that changed the way I saw my own business.

A few years ago, our business started scaling rapidly. Orders were up, revenue was growing, and we were expanding into new regions. But soon, problems followed:

- Misplaced shipments
- Confused team roles
- Unclear communication
- Customer complaints

We weren't failing due to a lack of effort; in fact, everyone was working harder than ever.

But we had no structure.

- No standard operating procedures.
- No automated inventory management.
- No delegation system for follow-ups or complaints.

Everything was in people's heads, and chaos was catching up.

That's when I decided to pause and build a structure. We didn't hire consultants or buy expensive software.

We started small:

- Created a **daily task checklist** for each department
- Designed a **simple CRM** in Excel for tracking leads and clients
- Introduced a **weekly review meeting** — structured, timed, with clear outcomes
- **Delegated ownership** to team leads with accountability

Within 2 months, the noise had reduced.

- Complaints dropped.
- Team confidence rose.
- Most importantly, I could step back without fear, knowing the system would carry the business.

In traditional LALA businesses, we often see systems passed down quietly:

- The **munimji** maintains daily cashbooks
- The **dukaan setup** is optimized for maximum customer flow
- Even the **chai breaks** are timed to sync with customer patterns

This is a **structure, even if it's informal. And it works.**

> "Structure turns effort into outcomes. It makes the difference between chaos and compound growth."

The Lesson

Passion may build the business, but structure sustains it.

You can hire talent, outsource work, and scale teams, but you **cannot delegate clarity, consistency, and control unless you have systems.**

So, build a structure.

- Even a simple checklist is a structure.
- Even a whiteboard that tracks your week is a system.
- Start small. Improve it. Make it yours.

> Because structure is not a restriction
> — it's your freedom to grow.

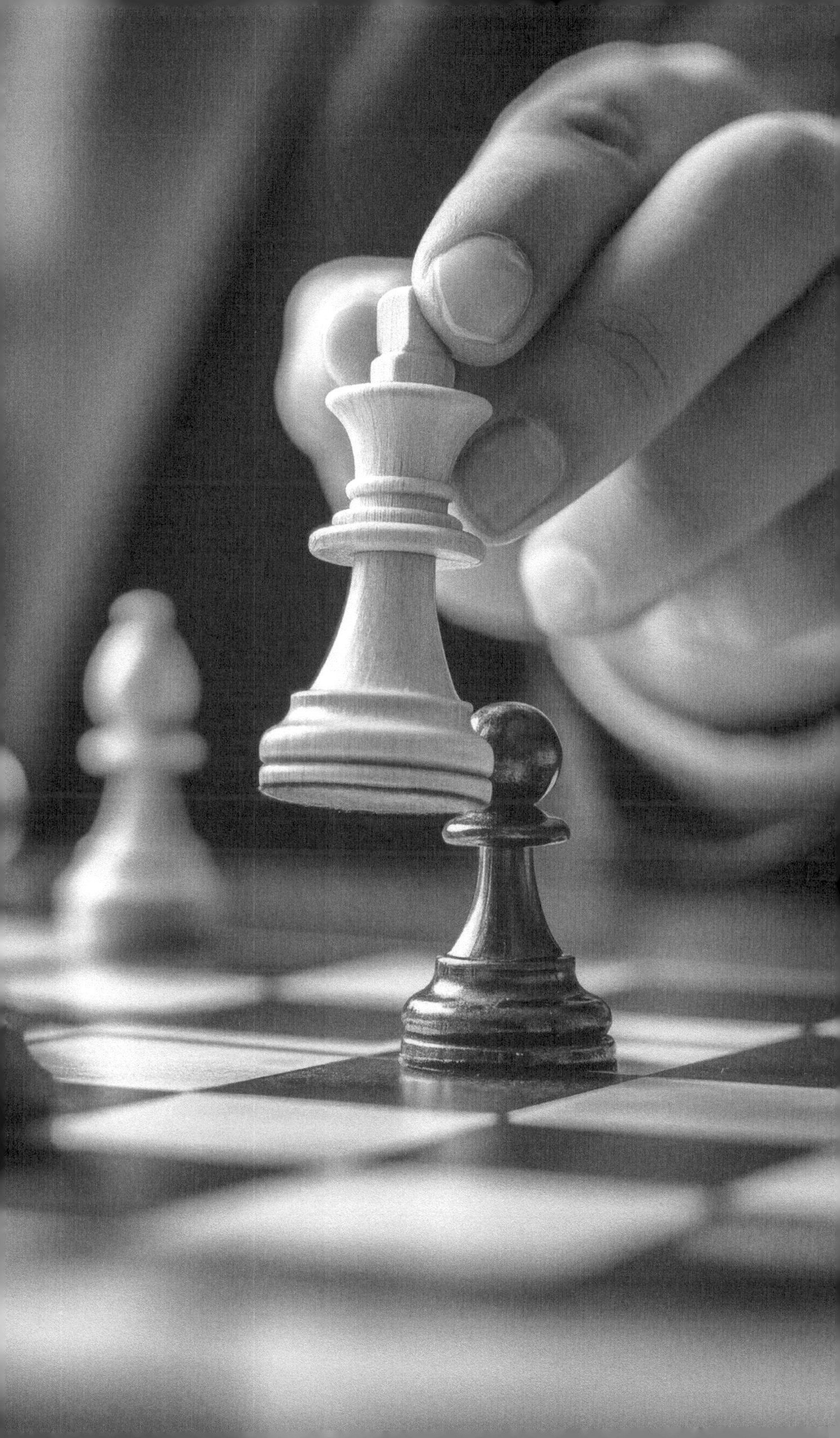

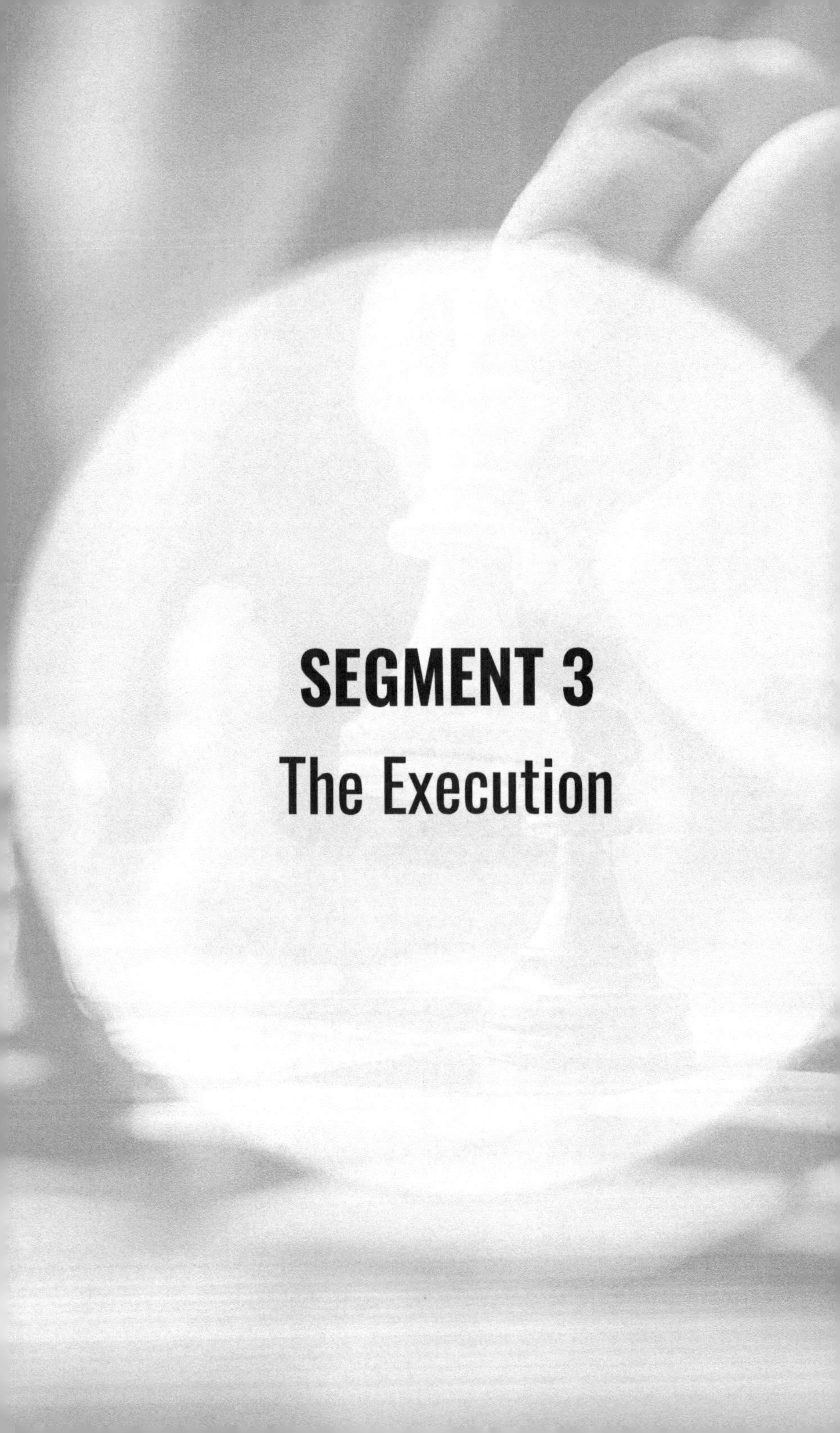

SEGMENT 3
The Execution

Market & Product Strategies according to the LALA Principle

Strategy in Action — Turning Wisdom into Wins

This section is where the timeless LALA mindset meets real-world execution.

After building the right foundation and transforming your thinking, it's now time to step into the battlefield of business with sharp eyes and a sharper strategy.

In these chapters, you'll learn how to spot invisible market opportunities and gaps that others miss, but the LALA sees first. You'll understand why doubling down on bestsellers is smarter than chasing trends, how innovation doesn't always mean invention, and why clearing dead stock is not a loss, but liberation.

We will also dive into the power of staying alert to your competition, the difference between growth and profitable growth, and how focus and daily discipline are the real engines of long-term success.

This segment equips you with practical, battle-tested tools to make better decisions, not just for more turnover, but for stronger margins, brand trust, and lasting business.

Because the LALA doesn't just play the game: He learns how to win it, on his own terms.

CHAPTER 23

Always Find Gaps in the Market & Fill Them

> ***"Don't find customers for your products. Find products for your customers."***
>
> ***– Seth Godin***

Opportunities don't always knock. They don't even shout. They **whisper.**

And it's the *Lala,* the one grounded in the market, who learns to hear that whisper.

In traditional Indian business culture, many great successes didn't come from inventing something completely new. They came from **noticing what was missing**, often before anyone else did.

- The Lala doesn't just ask: *"What can I sell?"*
- **He asks:** *"What is the customer struggling to find?"*

The Power of Market Gaps

In the early days of our business, I spent time visiting retail counters myself. I wasn't selling, I was listening. One day, I noticed several shopkeepers asking competitors for a particular product in a smaller size, but no one stocked it.

I asked one of them, "Why not?" He said, *"Customers are asking for trial sizes. But no one's making them."*

That was it — a whisper, not a shout.

We worked quickly to create a sample-sized version of our product. It wasn't easy, costs were higher per unit, and packaging needed tweaking, but we did it.

Within a month, sales spiked, especially in Tier 2 and 3 cities where affordability matters.

And here's the best part: many customers who tried the small pack came back for full-sized ones later.

That one gap opened up a new entry funnel and long-term revenue.

Another time, a dealer mentioned he was losing customers because people couldn't find bundled offerings, like combo packs for weddings or festivals.

Competitors were selling single units.

We bundled items, added festive branding, and launched limited-time "Celebration Packs."

We didn't invent a new product.

We just filled a gap in the customer experience.

The results?

Higher order value, seasonal buzz, and new shelf space in stores.

How to Spot Gaps like a Lala

- Walk through the market. Don't just call.
- Ask your retailers, "What are people asking for that you don't have?"
- Listen to complaints — there's opportunity in every frustration.
- Watch your competitors, but don't follow. *Observe what they're missing.*
- Look for seasonal, regional, or demographic-specific demands.

Often, a gap isn't about the product, it's about **how it's priced, packaged, positioned, or delivered.**

The Baniya mind doesn't chase trends — it tracks pain points. And wherever there's pain, there's profit — if you solve it well.

The Lesson

You don't need to create something revolutionary. You just need to notice what's missing and serve it better than anyone else.

Find the gap. Fill it.

And the market will reward you, quietly, but generously.

CHAPTER 24

Introduce Best Sellers for Maximum Impact

"Do more of what works, and less of what doesn't."

Not every product in your catalogue needs to be a superstar.

However, every business needs **a few champions,** the products that **fly off the shelves**, that people recognize you for, and that carry the rest of your business on their shoulders.

In the LALA business philosophy, we call them our '***YODHA***'.

These best sellers do more than generate revenue — they build your brand, win shelf space, create customer loyalty, and open the door to other products in your portfolio.

A Lala doesn't try to sell *everything to everyone.* He finds what works and **doubles down on it.**

Our Bestseller Story

In our early days, we offered a wide range of SKUs. Some moved, many didn't. We kept juggling promotions, discounts, and inventory, trying to push multiple products, until we noticed something simple:

- One product was moving 10x faster than the rest.
- Retailers were asking for repeat stock before others sold even once.
- Customers were referring that product to friends.

Instead of spreading our energy thin, we zoomed in.

We refined the packaging. We slightly improved the formula. We built better margins. Then we created a simple campaign, posters, shelf talkers, WhatsApp creatives — **all focused on this one hero product.**

Within a quarter:

- Our overall revenue jumped
- Distribution widened organically
- Retailers started stocking our other SKUs with it as a "trusted brand."

That one bestseller became our brand ambassador.

Why Focusing on Best Sellers Works

1. **They reduce risk** : You already know they work.
2. **They simplify marketing** : One focused message is stronger than ten confusing ones.
3. **They build brand recall** : Customers start associating your name with quality and reliability.

4. **They boost retailer confidence** : When a product sells fast, shopkeepers want more of your line.
5. **They become your launchpad** : Once you gain entry with your bestseller, it's easier to introduce new products.

Optimize What Sells

Don't just sell your best sellers, sharpen them.

- Improve the design
- Tell better stories around them
- Bundle them with other products
- Create limited editions or festive packs
- Collect testimonials and share them

Instead of launching 10 new things, sometimes it's smarter to make one great thing unbeatable.

The Lesson

Find your heroes.

Support them. Promote them. Polish them.

Because one great product, done right, can unlock doors that a hundred average ones never will.

In business, it's not about how many products you have — it's about how many products people remember you for. In business, it's not about how many products you have — it's about how many products people remember you for.

CHAPTER 25

Continuously Try New Products & Scale Successful Ones

> ***"Experimentation is the engine of innovation."***
>
> ***– Elon Musk***

A smart Lala is always experimenting, but never recklessly. Innovation, in our world, is not just about launching the next big thing.

It's about a cycle:

- Try something new
- Test it in the market
- Refine it based on feedback
- And if it clicks, **scale it fast, but smart**

Not every idea will succeed. That's okay.

Because even the ones that fail will **teach you** something about your customer, your product, or your strategy.

Our Trial-and-Test Journey

A few years ago, during the monsoon season, we introduced a new line of waterproof packaging for one of our main products. It was a low-investment experiment. We offered it to just 5 distributors and tracked feedback closely.

Some loved it. Some said the cost was slightly high.

So, we went back, tweaked the material, and optimized the cost.

Two months later, we relaunched the refined version, and it **became our standard packaging** across 80% of our product line.

- Customers appreciated the durability.
- Retailers said it reduced returns.
- Distributors promoted it themselves.

All of this came from a single small trial.

The Smart LALA Innovation Model

1. **Start small** : Test in one region, with trusted partners
2. **Track response** : Don't go by gut alone. Collect real feedback
2. **Tweak fast** : Improve what didn't work. Keep what did
3. **Scale strong** : Once it's proven, go wide with confidence

Another example

We once introduced a premium version of an existing product — same core formula, but better packaging, higher price point.

- **Some scoffed:** *"Who'll buy this in our market?"*

- But we didn't roll it out blindly.
- We tested it in high-income pockets and **corporate gifting channels.**
- Within weeks, bulk orders came in.

Your customer segments aren't uniform.

Sometimes a new product isn't wrong — it's just **wrongly placed**.

Why the LALA Approach Works

- You're not betting the house, just dipping your toe
- You stay close to market realities
- You avoid large inventory risks
- You stay relevant and build a culture of responsiveness

The Lesson

Try often. Fail small. Learn fast.

And when you see something work, **scale like your future depends on it.** Because sometimes, one smart experiment can unlock your next major growth leap.

Innovation isn't loud. It's disciplined. It's systematic. It's repeatable.

In the LALA mindset, we don't fear failure, but we do respect process.

CHAPTER 26

Never Let Dead Stock Pile Up

> ***"Inventory is money sitting around in another form."***
> ***– Rhonda Abrams***

In business, unsold stock is like an **unspoken truth:** it lingers in corners, drains your resources, and eats into your focus.

Every smart Lala knows:

- **Stock must be rotatedCash must be circulated Space must be liberated**

Dead stock is dangerous because it hides in plain sight. You look at it every day and say, *"Maybe next season."* Or, *"Let's wait a bit more."*

But while you're waiting, it's costing you rent, cash flow, shelf space, and mental energy.

A Lesson in Letting Go

I remember a batch of products we introduced that simply didn't perform.

The pricing was right, the quality was solid, but the **market didn't respond.**

We kept it in storage, hoping demand would pick up.

Six months later, not a single new order.

Meanwhile, newer SKUs were running short because we didn't have storage space.

That's when my grandfather gave me a simple piece of advice:

> *"Bikta nahi hai toh nikal do .*
> *Dukaan par barkat nahi hoti"*
> ("if it doesn't sell just liquidate shopdoesn't yield profits")

So we cleared it, bundled it into combo offers, offered discounts to loyal retailers, and even donated some units to build goodwill.

We took a small loss, but freed up cash, space, and mental clarity.

Within two months, we restocked fast movers, increased sales by 18%, and launched two new lines with the recovered resources.

That dead stock had been slowing our entire engine, silently.

Why You Should Move Dead Stock Quickly

1. **It blocks cash** that could be used for better inventory
2. **It wastes space**, physical and psychological
3. **It slows rotation**, affecting supplier credit terms
4. **It demotivates teams** who see clutter and failure
5. **It limits risk-taking**, because your capital is frozen

Holding on too long is not a strategy — it's denial.

LALA Approach to Inventory: Rotate or Eliminate

- **Track aging stock monthly** — anything beyond 60–90 days needs attention
- **Create clearance bins** — even at cost or zero profit
- **Bundle dead stock** with fast movers as deals
- **Offer stock to distributors as free add-ons**
- **Use it for samples, events, or charity** to build goodwill

And then? Move on.

Because every product that doesn't sell **clogs your future.**

The Lesson

Don't let dead stock gather dust and drain your ambition.

Clear it. Learn from it. And free up your resources to **chase what's working.**

> A smart Lala doesn't attach ego to every product.
>
> He knows — not everything you create will succeed. But everything you hold onto too long will slow you down

CHAPTER 27

Stay Updated with Your Competition

> ***"In business, the competition will bite you if you keep running; if you stand still, they will swallow you."***
>
> ***– Victor Kiam***

A smart Lala knows that **the market is a battlefield**, and everyone playing in it is both a rival and a reference point. That's why one of the oldest teachings in business is:

> *"Apne maal se pehle, doosre ka maal dekho."*
> ("Before checking your own goods, study what others are offering.")

This isn't about copying. It's about staying alert. Because in business, standing still is the fastest way to fall behind.

Competition Is Your Free MBA

Your competitors:

- Mistakes can **save you money**
- Wins can **inspire new ideas**

- ➢ Strategies can **reveal market shifts**
- ➢ Pricing can **warn you of upcoming pressure**

You don't need to spy or obsess.

You just need to **observe with intent**.

A Story of Sharp Awareness

A few years ago, one of our competitors started offering a bulk discount on a product we both sold. At first, **our team panicked, "They're undercutting us!"**

However, we didn't react. We observed.

Over the next few weeks, we visited some shared retailers and found the competitor's packaging was cheap, leading to damages and returns. Customers were complaining.

We used that moment to do two things:

1. We slightly improved our packaging with no change in cost.
2. We highlighted the packaging difference in our communication — "Better protected, better delivered."

The Result?

- The Retailers came back.
- And the competitor eventually pulled back the scheme.

We didn't win by lowering prices, we won by raising value. But we only did that because we were watching, not sleeping.

Ways to Stay Updated: The LALA Style

- ➢ **Visit the market regularly** : not just your retailers, but theirs
- ➢ **Talk to delivery agents, salesmen, and even customers** : they always know what's moving

- **Buy and experience competitor products** : compare their pricing, packaging, and service
- **Keep screenshots, samples, and flyers** : create a small "competition wall" in your office
- **Set a monthly review** : "What did they do? What can we do better?"

Remember: They are watching you too. Stay one step ahead.

The Lesson

Your competition is your **mirror** — it shows you where you shine and where you're slipping.

Never ignore it.

Study it. Learn from it. Adapt.

> In today's world, the one who learns fastest wins, not the one who starts first.

CHAPTER 28

Focus on Profitability, Not Just Growth at a Loss

"Sales are a vanity metric. Profit is what matters."

In today's world, growth often gets the spotlight. Everyone wants to say, "We doubled our sales," "We added 1,000 new customers," or "We expanded into 20 cities."

But here's the LALA truth:

Revenue is vanity. Profit is sanity. Cash flow is reality.

It's easy to grow fast by giving discounts, selling below cost, or spending heavily on marketing. But if your margins are shrinking, and your cash is bleeding, you're not building a business, you're burning one.

The Trap of Growth Without Profit

I once met a young entrepreneur who proudly told me,

"We clocked ₹10 crore in sales this year!"

I asked,

"That's great — and how much profit?"

He paused.

Then said, "Actually, we're in a loss. But the brand is growing!"

That may work for a funded startup chasing valuation. But for most of us, especially those in traditional businesses, profit is the pulse.

If you're not profitable, you're vulnerable.

A Lesson from Our Early Expansion

In our third year, we expanded into three new regions at once. The sales numbers looked good.

But transport costs, extra manpower, delayed payments, and distributor commissions ate away the margins.

For six months, we were busy but stressed.

On paper, we grew. But in reality, our profits dipped sharply.

That's when we hit pause.

We pulled back from one market, renegotiated terms in another, and streamlined our operations.

We stopped chasing size and started chasing smartness.

Within two quarters, our net profits recovered, even though our sales were slightly reduced.

That was the moment I truly understood:

Turnover feeds ego. Profit feeds families.

The LALA Approach to Profit-Focused Growth

1. **Price with intention** : Don't undercut blindly. Add value instead.
2. **Watch your input costs** : Renegotiate regularly, track wastage.
3. **Monitor margins by product and region** : Not all growth is equal.
4. **Say no to bad business** : Big orders with bad payment terms hurt more than they help.
5. **Review credit cycles** : Delayed cash is dead cash.

The Lesson

Anyone can grow by giving things away.

But building a **profitable**, **sustainable**, and **respected** business takes courage, discipline, and focus.

> So don't fall in love with growth charts.
>
> Fall in love with your P&L.
>
> That's where real business is built — and where real peace lies.

CHAPTER 29

Always Aim to Double Your Target

> ***"Shoot for the moon. Even if you miss, you'll land among the stars."***
>
> ***– Norman Vincent Peale***

Thinking small keeps you small.

It limits your mindset, your energy, and your creativity.

But when you say, **"Let's double this,"** something changes. Your brain shifts gears. Your team sits up.

Suddenly, average isn't enough, and new ideas begin to flow.

The LALA mindset isn't just about survival.

It's about scaling with purpose.

Stretch Thinking Creates Smart Execution

Early in our journey, we were discussing our quarterly target – ₹15 lakhs.

We were on track.

But I threw a challenge to the team:

"What if we aim for ₹30 lakhs instead?"

At first, they laughed. Then they paused.

And slowly, ideas started to flow:

- "Let's re-engage dormant distributors."
- "Let's bundle slow-moving stock with fast ones to boost volume."
- "Let's do a limited-time offer on high-demand SKUs."
- "Let's visit 5 new towns where we haven't pitched yet."

We didn't hit ₹30 lakhs that quarter.

We did ₹24 lakhs.

Which was still 60% higher than our original goal and far beyond what we would've achieved without stretching.

You don't grow by hitting small goals.

You grow by pushing your thinking beyond comfort.

How to Apply the "Double It" Principle – LALA Style

1. **Set a realistic goal, then double it** for planning
2. **Build new systems**, not just more effort — think smarter, not harder
3. **Break it down** : doubling doesn't mean doubling *everything*; focus on high-leverage areas
4. **Rally your team** : people rise when they're challenged
5. **Track progress weekly** : adjust fast, keep momentum

Why It Works

- It **forces creative thinking**
- It makes you look beyond obvious customers
- It builds a culture of **ownership and hustle**
- It attracts more attention from the market
- It builds internal **confidence and capacity**

When you **aim higher**, your team **grows stronger,** even if the result doesn't double, the mindset does.

A Lala may start with *paise*, but he thinks in potential.

That's where real growth begins.

The Lesson

Don't fear big goals — fear small thinking.

Every time you plan, ask yourself:

"What would it take to double this?"

Even if you don't get there, you'll go **farther than you imagined**.

> Growth doesn't come from what you know, it comes from what you believe is possible.

CHAPTER 30

Success Is a Byproduct of Dedication & Focus

> ***"Success is the sum of small efforts, repeated day in and day out."***
>
> ***– Robert Collier***

In the world of business, people often chase the spotlight, the big numbers, the milestones, the fame.

But in the *LALA mindset*, we're taught a different truth:

> Success isn't something you chase.
> It's something you attract through consistent dedication and focus.

You don't have to be the smartest in the room. You just have to **show up every day,** with discipline, with purpose, and with the desire to improve, even 1%.

The Compound Effect of Small Efforts

When I started out, I didn't have extraordinary skills. But I made a personal rule:

"Do something useful for the business — every single day."

- Sometimes that meant visiting just one client.
- Sometimes it meant learning how to use Excel better.
- Sometimes it was reviewing stock movement late at night.

None of it looked glamorous.

But over time, these small actions compounded, and the results came quietly but powerfully.

Just like water dripping on stone, focus and effort shape your business over time.

A Story from Our Warehouse

There was a worker named Raju in our warehouse, not highly educated, not very talkative. But every day, he would arrive before time, clean the shelves, arrange goods with precision, and assist others without being told.

One year later, he was handling **logistics coordination**. Not because we promoted him, but because his **dedication created his own promotion.**

His story reminded me that **success never skips those who show up fully.**

Why Dedication Matters More Than Talent

- ➢ Talent without focus burns out.
- ➢ Intelligence without consistency produces inconsistency.
- ➢ Passion without patience becomes frustration.
- ➢ But **dedication with direction?** That's unstoppable.

The LALA Way to Build Focus

- **Stick to a morning routine** : how you start the day shapes how you finish it
- **Plan your top 3 priorities** every day : don't aim to do everything, aim to do what matters
- **Avoid distractions** : social media can wait; customers can't
- **Measure what matters** : track effort, not just outcome
- **Rest, but don't quit** : pace yourself, not punish yourself

The Lala doesn't seek instant results — he seeks lasting impact. And that comes only from long-term dedication.

The Lesson

Success is not an event.

It's a *result* — a **byproduct** of thousands of tiny, focused actions.

- Keep improving.
- Keep learning.
- Keep showing up.

> And one day, you'll look back and realize —
> **Success didn't come from chasing big goals.**
> **It came from never giving up on small ones.**

CHAPTER 31

Just Do It – "We Will Achieve Success"

> ***"You don't have to be great to start, but you have to start to be great."***
>
> ***– Zig Ziglar***

One of the biggest killers of business success is **overthinking.**

We keep planning, tweaking, discussing, and analyzing until the moment is gone, the spark is lost, and the opportunity has passed.

A true Lala believes:

> *"Pehle karo, fir sudharo — perfect toh ho hi jaayega."*
> ("Start first and fix later — perfection will follow.")

In business, **momentum is everything.** You don't have to get it perfect, you just have to get it going.

From Idea to Action — Quickly

There was a time when we were considering launching a new regional product line. The team wanted 6 months for R&D, competitor mapping, branding workshops, and pilot testing.

I agreed to the importance of planning. But I also knew the **window was small** — a competitor had just exited the region.

So we trimmed the plan to 4 weeks:

- Identified our top SKUs
- Repackaged with regional flavor and messaging
- Sent samples to key distributors with simple flyers
- Launched quietly but confidently

Within two months, we broke even.

Within six, we dominated the segment.

Had we waited for perfection, **someone else would've taken that spot**.

Action brought clarity. Speed created success.

Why Action Wins

- ➢ It creates feedback faster than planning ever could
- ➢ It builds team energy, people feel progress
- ➢ It scares competitors, while they're watching, you're moving
- ➢ It reveals real-world problems, and gives you time to fix them early
- ➢ It creates **confidence**, and confidence creates consistency

Inaction is expensive. Indecision is riskier than trying and failing.

The LALA Way: Think Fast. Move Smart. Execute Boldly.

- ➢ **Trust your gut :** when combined with ground research
- ➢ **Launch on a small scale :** test, learn, and iterate
- ➢ **Take calculated risks :** not blind leaps, but brave steps

- **Involve your team early :** collective momentum drives faster execution
- **Remember:** "Start now. "Knowledge becomes power only when applied."
- **Fix later."** Done is better than perfect.

The Lesson

Waiting for the perfect plan often means never starting. Instead, **believe in your preparation, trust your experience, and take the leap.**

Even a small step forward brings more progress than a big idea sitting on the shelf.

So repeat after me:
"We will achieve success."
Not when we start. But because we start.

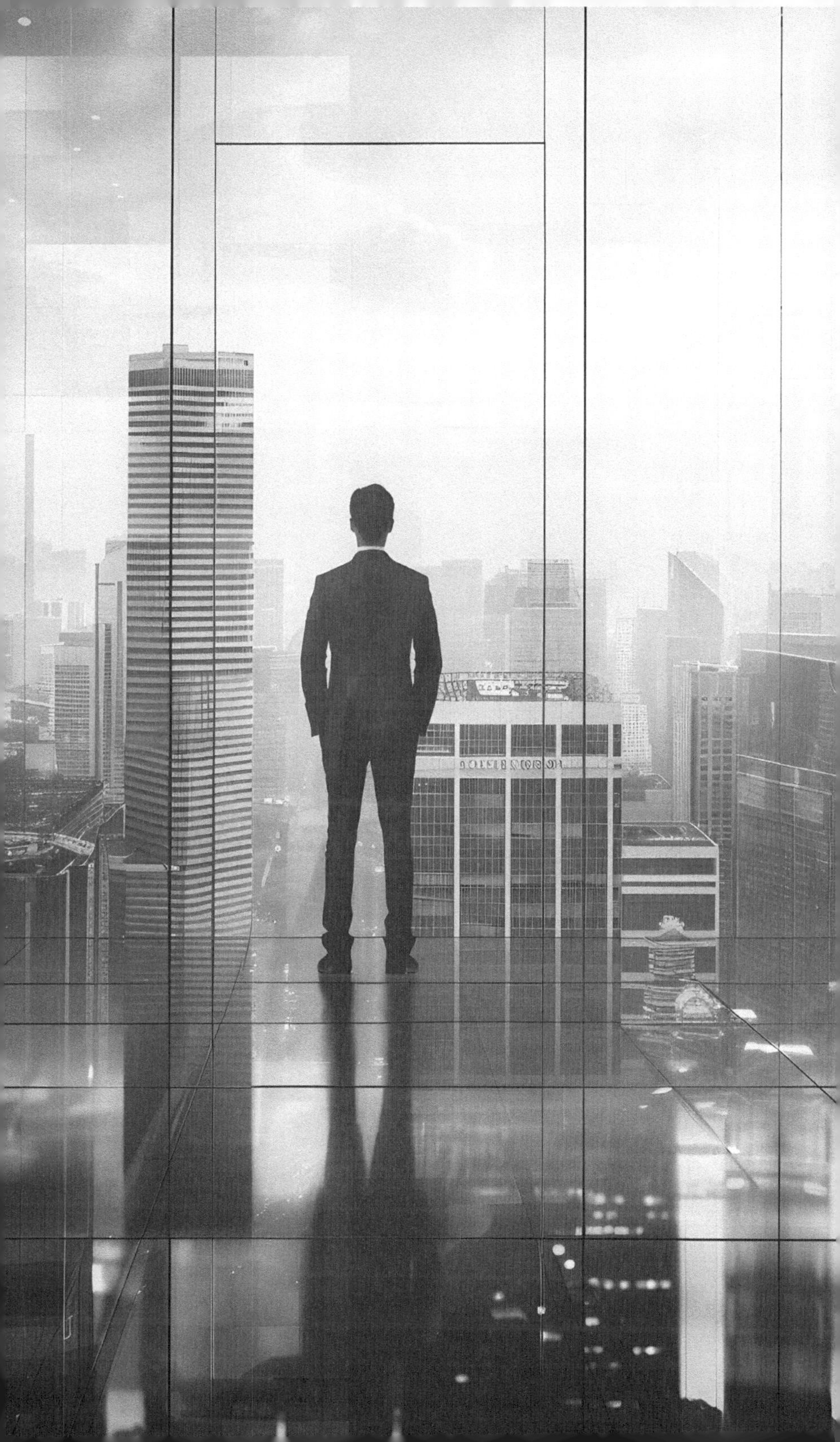

SEGMENT 3
The Conclusion

Reading this book is just the first step.

The real transformation begins when you take these timeless principles off the page and into your everyday business. The LALA Principles are not meant to be admired from a distance. They're tools meant to be used — sharpened by reflection, strengthened by practice, and refined by experience. This implementation guide is designed to help you live these principles in real time, one week at a time. Through simple exercises, honest self-checks, and small but consistent actions, you'll start seeing change where it matters most — in your habits, your thinking, your team, and your bottom line. Because in business, clarity without action is just noise. Let's turn knowledge into movement — and principles into results.

CHAPTER 32

A Heartfelt Note For My Readers

Dear Reader,

Thank you!

Thank you for taking the time to read *The LALA Principles.* Thank you for walking with me through stories of struggle, values, failures, wins, family, faith, and growth.

This book is not just about business.

It's about **a mindset** — one I learned from my elders, lived through experience, and shaped into something I now humbly share with the world.

If even one sentence made you pause, reflect, or feel more inspired, this journey has been worth it.

You are now a part of the LALA family — a tribe of dreamers who believe in building with **values, wisdom, grit, and grace.**

Always remember:

Success is not just about money. It's about meaning. It's not just about how far you go — it's about who you lift along the way.

Wherever you are in your journey — whether just starting out, growing a venture, or rebuilding from a setback — I wish you **courage, clarity, and endless opportunity.**

Keep learning. Keep adapting. Keep walking the LALA path — with your head high and your heart full.

CHAPTER 33

The Journey Continues

The LALA Principles is not just a book.

It's a piece of my heart. A reflection of my roots. And a roadmap built on real experiences, real people, and real values.

Through every principle shared, every story told, and every lesson remembered, my goal has been simple:

To show that success built on integrity, discipline, and relationships is not only possible, it is timeless.

In a world that often runs after shortcuts, hype, and noise, **the LALA mindset** brings us back to what truly matters:

- **Commitment over convenience**
- **Relationships over transactions**
- **Patience over panic**
- **Principles over profits**

Whether you're starting a business, running a family enterprise, or navigating life with entrepreneurial energy, know this:

You already have what it takes.

The strength, the wisdom, the instinct — it's in your blood, just as it was in mine.

And when you pair that with **learning, consistency, humility, and fire**, nothing can stop you.

> "In business and life, you don't just grow numbers — you grow people, trust, and legacy."

So keep going. Keep learning.

Live your story. Lead with heart.

And wherever your path takes you, **walk it like a LALA.**

With respect, passion, and pride,

Nitin Gupta (A LALA FROM INSIDE)

CHAPTER 34

Spark It Off –

"Knowledge becomes power only when applied."

Apply the LALA Principles to Your Business

Weekly Reflection Prompts

- What principle did I focus on this week?
- Where did I struggle to stay committed?
- How did I demonstrate respect for my customers or team?
- What did I learn that I can implement immediately?

Action Steps

1. Choose 1 principle to apply each week.
2. Write down 3 specific actions aligned with that principle.
3. At the end of the week, evaluate what worked and what didn't.

LALA Lab Exercises (samples):

- **For Commitment:** Write a list of promises made to clients/team—rate your delivery.
- **For Financial Discipline:** Track business expenses for a week. Identify 2 areas to optimize.
- **For Customer Respect:** Call your top 5 customers and ask for honest feedback.
- **For Innovation:** Choose one process you can automate or simplify this month.

Notes